DISABILITY PSYCHOTHERAPY

DISABILITY PSYCHOTHERAPY

An Innovative Approach to Trauma-Informed Care

Patricia Frankish

KARNAC

First published in 2016 by
Karnac Books Ltd
118 Finchley Road
London NW3 5HT

British Library Cataloguing in Publication Data

A C.I.P. for this book is available from the British Library

ISBN-13: 978-1-78220-316-2

Typeset by V Publishing Solutions Pvt Ltd., Chennai, India

Printed in Great Britain by TJ International Ltd, Padstow, Cornwall

www.karnacbooks.com

CONTENTS

ABOUT THE AUTHOR

Patricia Frankish is a Clinical Psychologist and Psychotherapist with many years of experience in the field of disability. Her doctoral study established a method for measuring emotional developmental stages in people, who had suffered trauma, and consequent interference in the developmental process.

She is from Lincolnshire and after working in a range of settings and spending six years in North Yorkshire and Teesside, she has settled back in Lincolnshire with her own business in partnership with her daughter. They specialise in providing services for people with complex needs, using the model that Pat has developed. They offer direct support, training and therapy, either as a package or one component. For those who need it they also provide accommodation.

Pat has been President of the British Psychological Society, was a founding member of the Institute of Psychotherapy and Disability and is an active member of her local Church and community.

PREFACE

This book has come to be written after a period of many years of trying to bring together the different theoretical positions of traditional psychoanalysis, plus a traditional understanding of learning disability and of my own experience. It seems appropriate to begin by placing this book in time and space although taking, to some extent, a post-modern position of accepting that time and space are constantly changing, constantly moving, and what is real for the individual is, just that, real for the individual. This work constitutes a collection of many hours of thinking, reading, soul searching, teaching, training and supervising, all based on clinical work with real people. The main teachers throughout this whole process have been the people: the clients who have put their trust in me as a therapist, and have demonstrated the enormous core strength that they have in the face of great adversity. Valerie Sinason (1992) has already written extensively about people with learning disabilities and the similarities and realities of their lives as they reflect on the basic human condition, the condition of being human as I see it. The condition of being human is constantly around for people with learning disabilities. Their lives have been, for many of them, almost inhuman, in that services for many years have treated them as a less than human group, and indeed in my early days of contact with the client group, they were referred to as sub-normal, in other words, not normal, below normal.

I want to say a little bit about my own life experience because that contributes to the way that I have studied and learned from other people's work, and have brought it together to the position that I now hold in relation to the work that I do. I grew up in the grounds of an old institution, in fact, it was called an institution when I was very small and became a hospital under the new National Health Service after 1948. My parents both worked at this hospital. It was a small 200-bed hospital in a rural community. As with many of these old institutions it was built in open countryside away from the general population. This particular hospital had been built by a benefactor as a "house of industry" prior to the workhouse days. It was converted to a work-house at the time of the workhouse being necessary and served quite a large geographical area at that time. There are reports that indicate that towards the end of its days as a workhouse there were a number of people who were imprisoned in chains or locked into rooms because they were considered to be mad or certainly not able to look after them-selves or be free to live in the community. And so, it was almost by default, as with many workhouses, that it became an institution for people who were at the time referred to as mentally defective. The term was later changed to mental sub-normality and that was the term that was in use in the days when I was a child. My mother was qualified as a registered nurse for the mentally subnormal and was a ward sister for much of my childhood. My father became the clerk and steward of the institution just before the Second World War and at the time of it being changed in to a hospital, he became the hospital secretary. They set an example for me, I think, of commitment, in that both of them stayed looking after people with learning disabilities until they retired. So, my father in fact served 46 years as the hospital secretary and my mother something less than that because she took time out to look after me, my brother, and my sister.

The hospital itself was, in the 1950s and 1960s, relatively self-sufficient in that there was land on which vegetables were grown and pigs were kept, and food generally was produced for the use of the hospital. Many people who lived there actually worked in the laundry or in the kitchen and were responsible for the cleaning and maintenance of the establishment. There was a rule at that time that men and women were not allowed to be in the same hospital because of the risk that they would get into relationships so in the hospital where I lived there were women and boys, but no men, which meant that the heavy farm work was probably less than it would have been at a different hospital that had catered for men.

My memories are of the women being dressed in very similar clothes. There were several shades of gingham, there was green and blue and red if I remember rightly and these dresses that the women wore were lined with a heavy cambric material. When I think now what it must have been like to wear, I find it quite distressing. They were herded together at mealtimes in big dining rooms. The huge rooms were heated by coke-burning stoves with big fire grates and fireguards at the end of each large room.

These are childhood memories of things that have stuck in my mind from those early days. I have very clear memories of my mother being a sister on a ward for children and seeing these little children, mostly boys—in fact initially they were all boys, girls weren't introduced until the 1970s I think—and these little boys in very serious states of organic brain damage, children with huge heads from untreated hydrocephalus, children who self-injured to such an extent that they were black and blue all of the time and there was very little that could be done to stop them. One little boy in particular I remember had a cot with a lid on because it was the only way that he could be contained at all. There were no wheelchairs for the children, there weren't even any chairs for the children, and on a sunny day, the cots would be wheeled out on to the grass so that they could have some fresh air. Again memories of a child.

These were situations I didn't really understand as a child. I knew that my mother worked hard. I knew that most of the people who lived at the hospital seemed quite content, we regularly socialised with them at the cinema that was brought in on an evening once a week, at the dances that happened again every week, at the tuck shop where we bought our sweets, and they bought their sweets. It seemed fairly normal to me because it was all I had ever known. I was teased at school for living at the loony bin, something that I didn't understand because I didn't know what loony meant and I didn't see the people that I saw every day as loony until somebody explained to me what it meant. But as I grew older I became aware that there were some people who lived in the hospital who were not content and who were seen as difficult, a nuisance, or bad and sometimes seen as dangerous.

I became aware of discussions about whether somebody needed to be sent to Rampton Special Hospital, which was the special hospital serving the area where I lived. I had this spectre, again a child's perspective, of Rampton Hospital being the last place on earth that anybody would ever want to go. The other thing I became aware of was that there were one or two people who occasionally caused a great deal of damage and threw tables and chairs and became very disruptive and destructive. They were given injections of some drug which I was told was haloperidol or paraldehyde which was used to control and calm them down.

I became aware also, as I moved into my teens, that the wards had what were called side rooms, what now would be called seclusion rooms, and these rooms were bare rooms with no handles on the inside of the door and people were put into these side rooms or were threatened with the side room if things were not going well. So as I became a teenager and moved through my teenage years I became somewhat more confused about whether or not this was the right thing to do for people to be looked after in this way and I began to question more and more whether in fact they would choose to live this way.

As it happened, I left home, following a reasonable level of discomfort with my parents and siblings, at sixteen, and moved away. I still went home every weekend and was aware still of changes, things that were developing, movements that were happening. Changes in the population of the hospital, in that it became acceptable in the 1960s that men and women could live in the same hospital and there were more girls admitted. The other thing that happened with this particular hospital was that they began to take more of the people with profound physical as well as learning disabilities so there was an increase in the population of very, very disabled people.

My own life took a turn in that I married very young and had three children. I remember very, very clearly during all three pregnancies thinking to myself that I mustn't have one of the children like the ones my mother looked after, but had no real understanding perhaps of what it could have meant. Nor were we in those days involved in any testing or screening process that would have indicated that we might have a disabled child. I was certainly familiar with children with Down Syndrome, hydrocephalus, spina bifida and some of the more distressing syndromes as well as some of the children who during the 1960s were very much experimented on medically in attempts to correct some of their difficulties. Some of the children that I knew did not live to the age of twenty.

In 1973, my marriage failed and in those days, there were very few choices for women with three children who needed a place of safety. The only real choice was for me to return to the parental home. My brother and sister had left to lead their own lives, my parents were on their own in a four-bedroom hospital house, and they had room for us. It was not an easy decision but we went, the four of us, and returned to live in the grounds of the hospital. I was in a position also of having no money and three dependent children and the obvious place to work was in the hospital.

For all the experience that I'd had of the place I had never worked there and faced the possibility with some trepidation. It was vitally important to me and my parents that no position should be created for me. I was appointed to a vacant position of "play leader". The job involved working with sixteen very disturbed adult women who were on a back ward where they were not allowed to leave the ward to go to occupational therapy or on outings because of their very difficult behaviour. They had a sort of pen that they could go into outside to get some fresh air and walk about but, generally speaking, were confined to the day rooms and the dormitories of the ward. I was given, as equipment to start this job, a diary, a notebook, a couple of pens, a ruler, a pencil, and a list of the 16 people—no toys, no materials, no ideas— and I suppose I was quite overwhelmed by this initially.

But, anyway, I went to meet the sixteen individuals and realised in fact their level of ability was less than my own children's in many ways. A number of them couldn't speak, all of them were ambulant, they could all run, and they could all fight, and they had a variety of antisocial behaviours. They were generally very unpopular with the nursing staff. I don't know where the idea came from because at that time, I had no scientific training at all but something told me that I had to find out what they could do. I had to try and find out where they all were in terms of level of ability in relation to each other.

So, I went to the occupational therapy department and borrowed one or two bits of equipment. These were some stacking cups, a screwing and unscrewing rod, a pencil and paper, and a nine-piece jigsaw. I took these things along to the sixteen people individually to see what their level of ability was on these tasks. I made a record of what they could actually manage and then divided them into four groups of four.

I secured the use of a little room at the end of the ward and decided that I would work with four at a time in this little room.

It became very obvious that I couldn't do anything with them unless I had some equipment and I managed to beg, borrow, and steal the first set of equipment, mainly from occupational therapy. I then managed to secure a small sum of money from central resources to buy some other bits and pieces of equipment. What happened, basically, was that the sixteen people each got an hour a day of one to four attention as opposed to having the whole day with, at best two to sixteen and frequently two to forty.

It was dramatic, the effect on these individuals and it was something that quite overwhelmed me at the time. They were people who had a very, very miserable and deprived life, their basic needs were met, they were clean and fed and they had somewhere to sleep but they had nothing to do and they had no joy in their lives at all. Given the opportunity to experience painting, drawing, playing, playing ball, and listening to music with a much better ratio of staff to patient resulted in some real achievements, some real benefits in terms of learning but even more so in terms of reduced antisocial behaviour.

It was about this time that a clinical psychologist in training came to our hospital as part of her placement. She came to our hospital one day a week for six months and it was obvious to her that the person who would be more likely to be able to work with her was me. She came and joined my groups initially and then we started to do some specific work with her with specific behaviour problems with individuals. She taught me how to work out whether somebody, through their own behaviour, was actually seeking attention or seeking affection and pointed out how important it is to know the difference. It's something that's stayed with me to this day because I hear so often people saying, "Oh, they're just attention seeking", and I get so cross because people wouldn't seek attention if they got enough attention. Quite often people are in fact desperately looking for affection and don't know how to get it.

The next stage of my working life led me into the development of a social training unit within the hospital to which many of my so-called hopeless cases did eventually graduate. They were able to attend sessions off the ward as they had become able to concentrate, to pay attention and use periods of time of up to an hour, enjoy them and, equally, benefit from them and learn new skills. There's one particular lady who stays in my mind very, very clearly who had a very, very antisocial behaviour of leaving faeces all over the hospital grounds. She would also wail and scream and make an awful lot of noise and was considered to be a very, very difficult, unreasonable, unlikeable woman. What we found in fact was that she was quite intelligent and that once she had something to do, something to interest her, some activity to take part in, she became almost a star pupil. The antisocial behaviour disappeared when she was able to gain appropriate adult-to-adult contact.

During the time of being in the social training unit, I became responsible for education. This was a very basic level of education, but I had also been asked if I would do some basic literacy work with some of the more able people who were on a different ward. I did that one evening a week for the education authority so I started to do a bit of very primary education with the more disabled people. I remember working with a lady with blocks and counting. If she had four blocks, she could add and subtract two plus two, two from four, two plus one, one from three. She was quite happy manipulating the blocks if she had four, but if you gave her five blocks she couldn't do anything with them at all, she couldn't even do the sums she had done with the four blocks. This absolutely fascinated me. I thought what is it about this lady, what is it about the way her brain works that won't allow her to retain the information about four if the message is confused with five. That was probably one of the most significant points at which I decided that I wanted to be a clinical psychologist. I wanted to understand what it is about the brain that lets it do some things and not others, that allows for pockets of ability within a very damaged brain at the same time as having huge areas of disability? Then to go back to the lady with the antisocial behaviour I mentioned a few paragraphs back, what it is about somebody that causes such antisocial behaviour and works against the possibility of making real human contact?

Around this time, I became quite ill myself in that I had an attack of acute arthritis which attacked nearly all of my joints and led to me being hospitalised on complete bed rest. The attack lasted eleven months. My children were largely looked after by my parents, it was a time of real shock for me, the time when I had to be dependent, something that I wasn't used to. A time of realising what it is like to be disabled, although for me it was temporary, but to realise what it was like to not be able to do what you want to do and to have to wait for things to come to you. The five weeks I lay on the bed in the hospital knowing I couldn't wash, go to the toilet, or eat unless somebody came within reach for me to ask then. Even when I had asked them, I had to wait for them to come back and attend to whatever it was that I needed. It gave me just a little bit of insight into what it must be like for people to spend the majority of their lives just waiting for something to happen, unless, of course, they make a tremendous fuss. Then something does happen, but usually it can become quite punitive.

The arthritis left me with permanent knee damage and very weak hands and wrists which meant that I could no longer work in a job that required such a high level of physical ability as the one I was doing. So, I had to leave the hospital and I became for a couple of years a registrar for births, deaths, and marriages. A very strange occupation but again it gave me an insight into people at times of major change in their lives, at the time when someone dies, the time when someone's born and the time they get married. Although as registrar you don't spend a lot of time with the people that you see, you are certainly face to face with very real emotion with everybody that you do see.

During the time that I was registrar, I continued my studies and planned to get a degree with the Open University. I had maintained contact with the clinical psychologist who had visited the hospital and she said to me one day, "Why don't you go to university?" to which I replied that people like me, that is, adults with growing children, can't go to university. Also, I'd left school without A levels and could not see that I had the entry requirements. Anyway, she encouraged me to apply and I wrote to Professor Alan Clark at Hull University, explaining what I wanted to do and why. He wrote back, by return of post, which was something that stays in my mind, inviting me to go to see him. I went to see him and he offered me an unconditional place to study special psychology at the University of Hull.

I then discovered, much to my surprise and delight, that my local authority in those days would pay me a maintenance grant for myself and my three children, and my travel expenses to allow me to go to the university without having to leave the children with someone else or move and take them with me. It felt like all my birthdays had come at once and it was a tremendous opportunity.

I was in my late twenties by this time, I had three growing children, constant financial difficulties, my physical health was below par, but I had an opportunity to do something I really wanted to do. So, I did my degree at Hull. I used to travel by car to the station, by train to the boat, by ferry across the Humber and by bus to the university. It was a constant and regular joke that the only thing I didn't do was fly. But I really enjoyed it. I remember most of what I was taught and I secured the upper second-class degree that I needed to go on to clinical psychology.

For my third-year project, I did a study of a child back in the hospital where I'd grown up. This was a child with cerebral palsy who, as far as I could see, did not have the level of learning disability that people assumed. The study involved a highly in-depth assessment of her ability and resulted in her getting an electric wheelchair and also developing an electronic communicator. I worked with the psychology department and the electronics department to develop one of the first talking phrase books. We put in nine phrases that could work by pressing a button of an adapted calculator. The machine would talk for her if she pressed the right buttons. It made such a huge difference to her life. I didn't pursue that line, although with some regret, but I am pleased that now the talking phrasebooks are readily available for people with learning disabilities.

One of the things that gave me in terms of my education, perhaps more than anything else, was an understanding of the system that worked against a child with a learning disability actually getting what they really needed. When we took her for her assessment for her electric wheelchair we arrived at the assessment centre and a complete stranger came up behind her, got hold of her wheelchair and wheeled her into the room with the doctor. She didn't know who it was; she didn't know where she was going, or what was going to happen. Consequently, she was in complete spasm by the time she actually got to the doctor and he said, "No way can she have an electric wheelchair, she will not be able to control it."

I was in a situation where I had no status but I had a voice and I said to him, "Please will you let her try, I know she can do it," and he looked at me and said, "Oh, all right then." We went through in to the workshop and put her in to an electric chair and showed her how the controls worked. She pulled the lever towards her and went backwards instead of forwards which didn't matter, and the smile went from ear to ear on her face and he said, "Okay she can have one." It was just so much a reflection of who's there, who's saying what, who's fighting, who's advocating. It really emphasised how powerless the individual is in that situation unless there is somebody there who can speak up for them. It was a very humbling experience.

What I found later though, which was even more distressing than some of the other things that I had experienced as this stage, was that when I went to visit her I would find that her electric wheelchair was switched off and that in fact it had been switched off because she was a nuisance. She was going where she shouldn't go; she was running away basically, or running into people or generally being mischievous. I reflected on what it would be like if somebody just suddenly said you can't walk, you're not allowed to, and I had memories of what that had been like for myself. It again reflected for me the complete power imbalance for people with learning disabilities that they can only move about when somebody says they can move about. It seemed so completely wrong to me.

The communicator was another issue. We developed a communicator for her that would actually speak sentences, become an electronic phrasebook, but she was not allowed to have one unless she could prove that she could discriminate between yes and no. She could discriminate between yes and no without a communicator and so wouldn't comply with any of the tests of this ability. It had memories for me of *Annie's Coming Out* (Crossley & McDonald, 1980): the young Australian girl, Annie, was able to use a communicator but absolutely refused to do it as a demonstration, would only use it if she had something she wanted to communicate. It shows tremendous spirit of the individual but is not helpful in terms of the individual being able to get what they want.

Despite my degree from the University of Hull, I was not able to secure a place on a clinical training course to continue straight on from university. What I did gain, however, was a place at Leeds Polytechnic for a postgraduate certificate of education to teach children with severe learning disabilities. I accepted that place with some trepidation, knowing that I wasn't really wanting to pursue a career as a teacher, but also realising that it was an opportunity to do some of the work that I wanted to do if I wasn't successful in becoming a clinical psychologist. I was also governed to some extent by the financial consideration in that I still had three dependent children and the course would attract a further year of maintenance payments from the local authority. So I did the course and I got tremendous pleasure and enjoyment out of working with the children. I learned an enormous amount about drama therapy, music therapy, the Derbyshire language scheme, physical therapy, all things that are so valuable in enabling children with learning disabilities to achieve their potential. I also learned that the school system is something that I find extremely difficult, as it seems that the school system exists far more for the school or for the education authority than it does for the children; it was yet another lesson for me in how difficult it is for systems to really accommodate the needs of individuals and I emphasise it here because it's very much a core part of the continued development of my thinking about the relationship between people and systems, and systems and people.

I faced the prospect of becoming a teacher within that system with some dread but at the same time could see that I would enjoy the work with children. I certainly enjoyed seeing and experiencing children learn because of the contact that is possible in the small classes that are provided in the special schools. But as it happened, I was able to secure a place for clinical training to start immediately after the end of the teaching certificate. This was a clinical training place at Liverpool University. It was a difficult decision to go and take up the place because my children were growing up and couldn't be moved for the two years that was involved. They were in school, at critical stages in their school-ing, and this had to be taken into account.

I had married again and decided on balance that the best thing to do was for me to go to Liverpool Monday to Friday and my husband, with the assistance of my mother, kept things going at home. It was a difficult decision and it was very costly, physically, mentally, finan-cially, emotionally. My knee gave up before the end of the course and I ended up having a cartilage removed and doing my viva in Liverpool Royal Infirmary. My marriage failed as my second husband had met somebody else by the time I'd finished the course, and I finished the course with a huge overdraft. With hindsight, I think it cost my children far more than I expected and I will for ever be grateful to them for the fact they did not say anything or complain in any way until after I'd returned.

The Liverpool course suited me extremely well. I had a breadth of experience of life that was quite different from my colleagues who were primarily academic in their background. This caused some difficulties for the group but the course certainly suited me. They'd made a com-mitment to being very eclectic, to opening our minds towards possible therapeutic avenues and to give us a solid grounding in being able to be clinical psychologists. There was an optional extra course in psycho-therapy which I took advantage of. I didn't at that stage know what psychotherapy was, but I learned very quickly. As it happened my first referral in my first placement turned out to be a gentleman with a borderline personality disorder. Because I had formed a therapeutic relationship with him by the time I had finished the assessment, I was allowed to continue to see him. I organised supervision and I did in fact see him for the whole two years that I was in Liverpool, giving me the benefit of long-term therapy with supervision. This is something for which I shall be eternally grateful.

There was a further unusual twist in that in my second placement I formed a therapeutic relationship with a young man who worked almost entirely within dream material for the first few months of therapy. Again, I was allowed to keep him on for a year of therapy with supervision. These two experiences within themselves were invaluable in shaping me as a therapist and enabling me to perhaps have the courage to recognise that no matter how disturbed somebody is, if they are willing and able to work, their potential for growth is enormous. Their capacity and determination to use the therapeutic experience is a demonstration of their trust in another human being which in itself is core to their recovery.

Apart from the overall core value of the course, and the breadth of training, there was a third very significant experience for me during the two years. This was an opportunity to work psychodynamically with a child with a learning disability. When I went to do my learning disability placement, my supervisor was quite behavioural in orientation. I also did quite a bit of systems work introducing the Bereweeke (Felce, 1986) teaching skills system into a project which was very exciting work and again was a further part of my education in terms of looking at systems. But one day my supervisor said, "You are into this psychotherapy lark aren't you," to which I replied, "yes", and she said, "we've got this child who's very, very disturbed and we've tried everything behavioural we can think of as well as medical in terms of various medications and systems in terms of where he lived and who looked after him and so on and we can't get through to him at all, will you see him?"

I felt some reluctance because I was not qualified and I certainly hadn't tried psychotherapeutic techniques with children, never mind children with a learning disability. But, anyway, having discussed it with my supervisor and met the youngster I decided that after some more reading and following up the available information that I would consider this. The little boy was so distressed with himself. He couldn't keep still, he kicked, he spat, he stole food, he didn't sleep, if his clothes needed to be changed it took two or three staff. He was so beside himself with distress and he looked tormented, there's no other word to describe it.

So having met him I went away to read some of Melanie Klein's work (1922) and followed her instructions about the therapeutic space and the therapeutic toys. I assembled a box of Kleinian toys and arranged to have a room that was relatively bare, apart from a couple of chairs and a table, to work with this little boy. I arranged ten sessions. The first day that he was brought to the therapy room, the door was closed, and it was just him and me; he immediately started to try to convey to me what it was that was bothering him. I was so moved by the fact that this little boy, who didn't know me, could recognise therapeutic space when it was there, could recognise that somebody was wanting to help him. He had no verbal language, he had a wide variety of mannerisms, was very, very active. He used the toys, gestures, eye contact, and physical contact to try to make me understand what it was that was going on in his head. And, following the ideas that I'd read in Melanie Klein's work, I interpreted his behaviour, his mannerisms, his gestures. If I'd got the interpretation right, he would look at me and the behaviour would stop. Then he would go on to something else.

During the ten sessions, he dealt with some very, very horrible life experiences, but, more importantly, he discovered that another human being, that is, me, was both willing and able to listen to him. It was listening with eyes rather than ears. I was able to talk to him and label his distress in a way that he could use and could tolerate. That seemed to be what we were doing, in fact, finding a way that this youngster could tolerate what had happened to him and could tolerate being with another human being. It seemed to be that so long as the other human being could tolerate what had happened to him then so could be. And that was the beginnings of my belief, which I think is the right word, in the psychoanalytic tradition in working with people with a learning disability and is the major part of the introduction to this book.

The next stage after qualifying and starting my first job as a fledged qualified clinical psychologist was to consider the ethics of using a technique that was not proven, not tested. I started my first job with people with learning disabilities in a community setting unclear in my own mind about whether in fact I would continue to use the approach. What I found very quickly were two things. One was that the referrals that were coming my way were of people who were very disturbed and for whom traditional approaches had not been effective. They were certainly giving all the visible signs of having some internal emotional distress and trauma. Also, there was nothing in the literature to indicate that it was wrong to use psychotherapeutic approaches with people with learning disability, merely that it was pointless. As I'd had experience that indicated that it wasn't pointless, I continued to work with individuals from the orientation.

At the same time, I decided that I was quite isolated and I wanted to make contact with other people with similar approaches. I made contact with people within my local geographical area and we formed a peer supervision and support group, primarily clinical psychologists with some other professions involved. That support group was a mainstay for our development over a number of years. It was during one of these support sessions that I was introduced to the work of Margaret Mahler (1979) and this has been a major influence in my work ever since for two significant reasons. The first is that I find Margaret Mahler's work so entirely relevant to everything I come across in my learning disability work; second, because her approach to recognising and analysing emotional difficulties relates very much to the system as well as the individual. It allows for a systemic approach to treatment. You will find as I go through the work that this is a recurrent theme. People do not exist in isolation and people are affected by the environment in which they find themselves and in my view, they cannot be separated. It has led to me questioning the one to one therapy model and particularly the pure psychoanalytical models. It has led to me blurring the boundaries between psychology and behavioural understandings. What I think it has done is to provide me with a framework of understandings that has universal value and I will endeavour to develop this theme further.

Some of the early work has been published in scientific journals. What has happened from there is that I have been involved in a lot of clinical work, a lot of teaching, supervision of other people, a lot of collaboration with other people on models of understanding, ways of working, not all clinical psychologists, often a range of different professions, I have broadened my interest and peer group to people working in other European countries and in the Americas. I have endeavoured to make contact through attending the IASSIDD (International Association for the Scientific Study of Intellectual and Developmental Disabilities) World Congress and joining the European Association for Mental Health in Intellectual Disability (MHID) to share my thinking and learn from other people's thinking in order to further develop the theoretical position I now hold.

The rest of this book is an expansion of the theoretical position based on some very traditional authors but applying all of the traditional work to the client group of people with a learning disability. I've attempted to gather together some of the significant life experiences in relation to people with learning disabilities that have helped me to have an open mind. I've tried to get closer to a way of understanding that meaning. What follows in the next few chapters is an exploration of the work and writings of some key analysts whose work has, in my view, contributed a great deal to this understanding of meaning. The main authors covered are Winnicott, Bowlby, Klein, and Mahler with contributions from Freud, Malan, Bion, and of course Sinason. What I've tried to do is capture what they found in their own clinical work and relate it to the known life experiences of people with learning disabilities, together with some of the expectations we might have of what those life experiences have been. The implications then are summarised from time to time throughout the chapters but will be summarised at the end in relation to how we use this information in order to work beside and for people with learning disabilities.

CHAPTER ONE

Winnicott

In this chapter, we begin to look at how the theories and ideas around child emotional development have been adapted. There will be an overview of some of the key ideas of Winnicott's work, which perhaps have had the most fundamental influence on my thinking in the work with people with learning disabilities. My development of the trauma-informed care (TIC) model recognises that the delicate process of emotional development may be impacted upon in children with disabilities, due to their very disability. This can have fundamental, life-long effects on a person's functioning which leads to them experiencing "compounded" difficulties over and above the original disability they were born with.

Donald Winnicott was born in 1896 and died in 1971. His work was mainly with children and he was one of the "second generation" of psychoanalysts building on the ground breaking theoretical understandings that had been developed by Freud and Klein. He was very committed to teaching and training, not just to other therapists, but to passing on his ideas to the general public. During World War II, he had regular broadcasts on the BBC, in which he helped families to understand and cope with the difficulties of children being separated due to evacuation, fathers being absent due to fighting in the war and also

1

death and bereavement for those who had lost family members. His style was easy to follow and understand. Consequently, there are many publications, made up not only of his academic writings, but also collections of the broadcasts he made (e.g., 1971a, 1971b, 1990).

In *The Child, the Family and the Outside World* (1973), which was a collection of his BBC broadcasts, Winnicott talks about what is needed for optimum emotional development. The underpinning concepts are that good enough mothering and the mother's maternal devotion are key to the child's personality development. This maternal devotion is especially concentrated in the first few weeks of life but also vitally important throughout the first few years of life. Winnicott very much stressed that this devotion could not be bought or imposed, but rather was "just there", an instinctual drive that arises after the process of pregnancy and giving birth. This has more recently been expanded by Gerhardt in *Why Love Matters* (2004). Today, with a wider range of people providing nurturing the phrase "good enough care" may be more acceptable. However, even if the mother is working, the availability of maternity leave means that the mother, in the majority of cases, is still likely to be the primary carer in this early period of life, and therefore the person with whom the child makes their first primary relationship.

Winnicott was very much writing in his time, reflecting the predominant traditional roles and societal structure. In more modern times, his ideas have attracted criticism in the fact it seemed to suggest that women were to blame when things went wrong. A number of clarifications need to be made to acknowledge these criticisms which otherwise may interfere with the reading and processing of the material here.

First, Winnicott was formulating his ideas and writing at a time when societal expectations were that the mother would be the main carer of the child. Today a wider range of people may have this role and the term "carer devotion" may be more appropriate. However, for the sake of simplicity and to follow in the spirit of Winnicott's ideas the term "mothering" will be used in this chapter, with the acknowledgement that this devoted care can be delivered by a "carer", as long as it is a consistent person with whom the child will develop their first-ever relationship as a human being.

Winnicott, rather than blaming the mother if emotional difficulties arise, was suggesting that if things are right, if a mother is supported to give the devotion that is natural and instinctual, without any intrusions or difficulties from the outside world in the earliest most concentrated stages, then this would be the best thing a child could have. Winnicott stressed that mothers and carers can be helped to recognise the importance and value of this devotion and can be supported to fulfil that role for their child.

It has also been felt that working mothers were being blamed for needing to work and therefore not being available for the child. However, Winnicott was very much making the point that the devotion of a mother, if it is there, is deeper than any social reality and is strong enough to sustain other difficulties, such as the parents needing to work.

This concept of maternal devotion is so immense that it has caused many defensive reactions. Psychoanalytic thinking has often attracted animosity due to the suggestion seeming to be that people are made bad by their experiences and consequently, someone is to blame for those experiences. This often elicits powerful defensive thinking in individuals who may be unable to bear this idea in relation to their own experiences or to those of others in their lives. This chapter, and indeed this whole book, is certainly not intended in any way to blame. Rather, by examining the factors that help things to go right, these factors can be used to provide an environment for people, not just in early life, but also later on, where a person's emotional development, even if it has been stunted, can be facilitated.

The first few months—factors in optimal development

In this section, we will outline some of the key elements Winnicott identified as needing to be present for an optimum emotional development. Later, consideration will be given to how a child with learning disabilities may be more vulnerable to disturbance of this process. However, it should be remembered that the aim of this understanding is that the disturbed parts of the process can be addressed, even in later life, to enable the individual to progress in their emotional development.

Winnicott very much emphasised that a baby is born with the drive and the ability to grow and develop, but needs to be provided with a suitable physical and emotional environment in which this development can occur. Winnicott called this the facilitating environment. The good enough mothering, and maternal devotion, provides this facilitating environment by enabling the child to have a relationship where it experiences the love, safety and security needed for emotional development to occur optimally.

With a newborn baby, maternal preoccupation hopefully occurs in the first few weeks of life when the mother is completely preoccupied with meeting the baby's needs. The mother becomes "tuned into" the baby so she becomes able to determine that a certain cry means hunger or a certain expression means the nappy is being filled. The pair are completely enmeshed to the extent Winnicott said "there is no such thing as a baby—but a nursing pair", in that the pair are, at this point, interdependent and the baby cannot survive without the food, love, security, and affection the mother is hopefully able to provide. The baby is not passive in this process, indeed it is the baby's energy that means the mother will respond to his needs, that is, by crying or looking a certain way.

At this stage, the child is only able to experience the world as this enmeshed relationship and is unable to distinguish that he is separate from his mother. Because the mother is preoccupied with meeting the baby's needs, the child's sense is that he is at the very centre of existence, or as Winnicott termed it, the child feels he is omnipotent. During this stage, the child's dependence on the carer is total.

The mother and child take part in what Winnicott termed "the dance of reciprocity" where mother and child will gaze into each other's eyes and will engage with each other. The baby will make spontaneous gestures or do something that the mother responds to, causing the baby to respond back and so on, giving the baby his first experience of interaction with another human being.

During this early stage of life, the baby experiences intense emotional states, as can be seen in any crying baby. The mother is driven by the intensity of this expressed emotion to seek the source of distress. It is extremely hard to ignore a crying baby, as the anxiety experienced by the parent is a reflection of what the child is experiencing at that moment. By seeking to find the source of distress and dealing with it, the carer is helping the child to process his emotional states, as he is unable to do so himself.

Winnicott uses the term "holding" to describe how the mother is literally emotionally holding the baby together, as a whole integrated being, in an integrated mental state, before the baby can do it. Winnicott described how the baby, because he is frightened, hungry, screaming or distressed is literally emotionally "falling apart" and that he relies on the fact that the mother or carer will not fall apart, that they will be able to hold on and tolerate the extremes of emotion that the child will gradually begin to learn to tolerate himself. In the book *Why Love Matters* (2004), psychoanalyst Sue Gerhardt examines the neurological evidence showing that this process helps to develop and set the neural pathways that are connected to emotional functioning. Although this new research is coming from a different perspective, it supports the ideas Winnicott spoke of many decades earlier.

It is through repeated experiences of having his needs met and his total dependence tolerated, that the child is able to begin to develop a sense of self. Winnicott described how the child "sees himself reflected in his mother's eyes". Hopefully, the baby will see the mother's love and joy reflected back. It is this loving, positive feedback, as well as having his complete dependence tolerated, his needs met and emotions regulated, in an overall environment of consistent love and security that enables the child to integrate his initially overwhelming sensory experiences into a sense of self or his ego. These positive experiences will enable the child to develop a sense of being a "good enough" person.

The majority of the baby's early experiences are around the primary functions—feeding, excreting, touch, and warmth. These functions, and them being attended to, assist in the development of the ability to emotionally "take in" and "give out". Winnicott describes how this sense and ability develops through the process of care received around feeding, drinking, and excretion. Winnicott describes how this process develops the sense of the relationship between the inside and outside world, both physically and emotionally.

As the baby gets a little bit older the mother naturally begins to move out of the maternal preoccupation stage as she begins to address some of her own needs and other demands on her. She may not be quite as tuned in to her child as she was previously and therefore may not meet his needs immediately. Very gradually, the mother and baby begin to move out of the enmeshed relationship. The child will feel extreme feelings of anger or frustration at not having his needs met immediately, at not being the omnipotent centre of the universe. However by soothing the baby, the mother, very gradually, helps the child to manage and tolerate these emotions in small, manageable chunks. Through this experience, the baby begins to realise that the mother is a separate being and begins the realisation that there is a world outside of the enmeshed mother and baby unit. The child begins to develop a sense of "what's me and what's not me", that is, the difference between himself and the outside world. All this helps to strengthen the sense of self or ego and is the foundation for developing independence.

The crux of the term "good enough mothering" is that it will not always meet the child's needs perfectly and in fact, those failures, as long as are manageable and bearable and don't totally overwhelm the child with fear or distress, are an extremely important part of the child's development towards independence and ability to tolerate disappointment and frustration.

Through receiving this good enough care and getting feedback that he is himself a "good enough child", the baby's ego is able to integrate further and the sense of self becomes strong enough for the child to be able to start relating to others. The child then begins to enter into relationships with others, usually the second parent first, siblings and then wider family members and friends. The baby is now emotionally able to explore his world, not only the other relationships available, but also the physical world. Because of the absolute trust the child has hopefully developed in his mother through the care he has received, the child monitors the mother's reactions for whether it is safe to explore in situations. Through these explorations the child begins to further reinforce the "what's me—what's not me?" boundary, that is, the difference between himself and the rest of the world. Through having received optimal care, the foundations have been laid to ensure the child is now on the path towards increasing independence and becoming a member of society.

Intellectual development

The capacity of the child to think develops through these explorations of the wider world. The baby begins to deal with and think about the information coming through his senses. The child progresses to being able to "think about" things, he begins to cathect, or hold in his head a reality of the world. When the child comes across something new, he relates this information to what is already being held in his head. The baby has reached the intellectual development stage that Winnicott called rationalisation, where he can think about himself and his own environment.

True self

Winnicott coined the term "true self" to describe how, if a child receives the optimal "good enough care", having his extreme dependence tolerated and his needs met consistently in a loving and secure primary relationship, then the sense of self the child develops is his true self. The child not only has a sense that he is "good enough", but his true self, or personality, develops and can be shown to the world.

This is the opposite to the experience of the child who has had to fit in with what the carer needs or wants and may have had to suppress his own needs for the convenience of others. The child may not have had his extreme dependency tolerated in a loving, consistent, or safe way. In this situation, the child may develop a sense of self that is not actually true of the child, but rather is a self that complies with the demands placed upon him. In this case, the child develops a false self, which is presented to the world. This can become so engrained over the early years, through the feedback he receives from others responding to this false self that the individual may have no sense of what has happened. The false self becomes entrenched as a way of defending or protecting the "true self" that wasn't responded to or nurtured.

Winnicott described how people who are able to develop and present to the world their true self naturally feel energised, creative, and glad to be alive and have a sense of "wholeness" or "completeness". Those people unfortunate enough to have developed a false self, unaware of the true self that remains defended, may have feelings of unreality or a sense of not really being alive and a feeling that happiness doesn't really exist.

Children with disabilities

So far, in this brief overview, Winnicott's key ideas regarding optimal emotional development have been presented. In children with disabilities, this process can be affected with consequences for emotional functioning later in life. The cornerstone of the Frankish TIC model is the acceptance and understanding of the many ways in which the emotional development process can be impacted upon. This can help to develop environments where these disruptions are understood and interventions put in place to try and address some of the issues.

If a child is born with an obvious disability, especially if unexpected, or due to birth trauma, this can be a time of unimaginable emotional upheaval for the parents. The perfect child, and his possible future that has been thought and fantasised about throughout pregnancy, has not arrived (Bicknell, 1983). The parents may initially be in shock affecting their emotions towards the child. In clinical practice working with people with disabilities in later life, it is not uncommon to hear that there was an instant rejection of the baby at birth, or at least a warding off of the usual attachment process.

The child may need to be in an incubator for a period. It is not uncommon to talk to parents whose children were born thirty or forty years ago and needed to be in incubators, who were told to go home and leave the baby in hospital care until the baby was ready to go home. Thankfully, modern neonatal medical practice now sees parental involvement as fundamental to the care of the incubated child. However, when an infant has needed to be in intensive care, even with the best possible care, there will have been some disruption experienced by the mother and child of the usual stage of maternal preoccupation and the pairs ability to tune into and develop a sense of each other. It is more likely that children with disabilities have to go into incubators than there are children who don't have disabilities. Clinicians in the learning disability field will have noticed the increasing numbers of people entering services who are premature baby survivors and needed special care.

A child needing medication for physical difficulties may have his senses dulled, as may a child with disabilities. This may be compounded if the child has both, meaning he may be less alert and less aware of who is there for him, less sensitive to the sounds that have become familiar in the womb such as the mother's voice and her smell. The baby may be less aware of the person providing the maternal devotion, of who is his mother. The baby's part in the early relationship may not be as active as the child without disabilities or not on medication, who is immediately looking for food.

As the disability is identified and the initial shock wears off, there can be immense tension and tumultuous emotions experienced by the parents, other family members, and medical staff caring for the child. Very difficult and heart wrenching decisions may need to be taken about care. As the reality of the situation begins to sink in, there can be tremendous despair, a grieving for the imagined perfect child who has not arrived. Hopefully there is love for the actual child who has arrived. The breaking of the news and the initial support of the parents will affect their ability to process the enormity of what has happened. There are undoubtedly many parents who have been told at birth that their child has a disability, whose love for the child has been greater than any of the other thoughts and emotions felt. However, there can be no doubt that the early reception of a child with disabilities is likely to be different to how a child without disabilities is received.

There can sometimes be, for an infant with disabilities, a great deal of tension and upset around the primary functions. The child may find it difficult to suck and feed. They may have to be tube fed, sometimes for many years. Various bowel conditions are commonly associated with people with a learning disability which may result in delay in establishing a bowel habit. In some conditions, invasive surgical procedures are needed, causing pain and discomfort. Disturbances in these primary functions can impact on the delicate process of emotional development around "taking in" and "giving out" of emotions.

The experience of being touched and held will be affected if the child is very fragile and needs to be in an incubator. Touch can also be affected if a child is fretful and therefore unrewarding for the parent to hold. More commonly, the child may be so quiet, maybe through medication or limited sensory awareness, that he appears settled, and gets handled a lot less because he doesn't cry and therefore doesn't get picked up.

Many clinicians will argue that at this stage the baby would be unaware of what is going on and would be unaffected by it. Winnicott would argue that the child would be aware. It is highly likely that there may be some disturbance of the optimal emotional development experience for the child, of the mother's ability to provide complete maternal devotion in a manner undisturbed by the outside world. The earliest stages of emotional development may have been interfered with.

There is now an increasing amount of research evidencing that babies in special care units seem to thrive better if they get more physical contact, and more close contact with their mother and other human beings from birth. Again, although from a different perspective, this is supporting the ideas Winnicott presented decades ago. Research from Romanian orphanages has been a rich source of data showing the improved outcomes for babies that received more human contact, either with staff or with another baby sharing their cot. Sue Gerhardt documents evidence showing the actual neurological developments that occur with touch and nursing and the detrimental impact neurologically of this being interfered with.

In this section, we have looked at some of the things Winnicott felt to be very important in the emotional development of a non-disabled child and how these may be very prominently affected in the experience of a disabled child, because of the very disability, and its impact on those around the child. We will now go on to examine some of the longer-term consequences of this disturbance in the delicate emotional development process for these children.

Fear as a possible consequence

A key theme running through Winnicott's ideas is that of the total dependence that needs to be recognised, accepted, and tolerated by the parents. If this is not possible, the child will feel rejected, resulting in many fears. Winnicott stresses that this early feeling of rejection always results in a fear of domination through the child's dependence needs not being met, but rather the child being required to fit in with the needs of the parent. His ideas about what may result from disturbance of this very early stage, the very early devoted relationship are very appropriate when applied to people with learning disabilities. Indeed, some people with learning disabilities may remain emotionally dependent, as they have not been able to develop through the disturbance in this early stage. Then, as they become older and those around them begin to have chronological expectations of them, they may have that dependency rejected throughout the majority of their lives.

Winnicott talked about a number of fears that may arise in a child from the experience of not having his extreme dependence tolerated, which would be the result of a failure in this early stage. The first fear he talked about was a long term fear of women, for both men and women, coming from the experience of the first woman that they relate to, failing to tolerate their extreme dependence. The second fear is of domination by everyone else leading to an anxious personality and becoming very compliant with authority. The third resultant fear Winnicott talks about is a fear of everything. This is where the child has had no sense of feeling safe from the beginning of their lives, with no one being able to tolerate their complete dependence and ending up afraid of everything. Because they have no experience of not feeling afraid, they consequently stay afraid forever and carry this sense throughout life.

How might this play out in an adult with learning disabilities? It is not uncommon to hear someone described as "oh he only likes to be looked after by male staff", the implication being that the person feels physically safer with the male staff because they are stronger and able to contain him (possibly through restraint) if necessary. Thinking about Winnicott's ideas, quite often this issue is due to a fear of female staff, a fear of what they may do. It is not uncommon to discover in the history of some very disturbed individuals, that they have been abused by women in the past and that they are very confused in their understanding of what is to be expected from a woman.

The fear of domination that Winnicott talked about may bring out, in someone with learning disability, a reaction that leads to them being permanently smiley or permanently nice, which has the effect of warding off attack from other people. Valerie Sinason (1992) has described this as the "handicapped smile" and this will be discussed in a later chapter. But from Winnicott's position, this way of behaving is an adaptive behaviour to cope with the fear of being pushed around or dominated by other people.

The fear of everything, that Winnicott talks about, can be seen in people with learning disability, who are often very, very frightened inside. They have a basic fear that there is nobody in the world for them, and often when gaining historical information it can be seen that there has indeed been no reliable, close, consistent relationship ever throughout their life.

A disturbance in the early nurturing relationship can also impact on the ability to "take in" and give out emotionally. If there has been a disturbance in the part of the nurturing relationship around feeding and excretion, it can lead to a stunting in the relationship between the inside and outside world. This can lead to eating difficulties as well as having other emotional impacts such as an inability to benefit from emotional contact, a very real superficiality in all contact and no real emotional growth of the inside self. This impaired ability to give out can lead to a person seeming very selfish and egocentric in that they can't ever consider what anyone else might need or want, they seem unable to do anything for anyone else or care about another. This could be phrased as an inability to have empathy for others. Bion (1959) talked about the notion of a person needing to be "thought about" in the early relationship to be able to develop the ability to think of others. This being "thought about" would be the fundamental part of having feeding and excretion needs taken care of and the difficulties may arise from receiving this in an "unthinking" way. For staff, such people can be very frustrating, but they are like that because there has not been sufficient nurturing of the "inside self". Therefore, there is very little on the inside, emotionally, for the person to invest in the outside world.

The child in the early days is totally dependent and the child with a disability may be totally dependent for a lot longer. Winnicott would argue that the degree to which these dependence needs are met and tolerated by the primary carer influences the emotional development of the child. If needs are not tolerated and met then the area of difficulty would influence the type of disturbance that may occur in later life.

This argument does put a huge amount of pressure on the primary carer in the first few months of the child's life. However if this argument can be understood and accepted in terms of what those needs of the child are, then we have an obligation as a society to help support and facilitate mothers and primary carers in this vitally important societal role and very much especially those who are finding it difficult. If we ignore or under support this vitally important process then we are creating enormous difficulties for the future.

The role of the family

In his book *The Child, the Family and the Outside World* (1973), Winnicott moves on to a description of the impact of the wider family, not only on the process of the early stage of total dependence but at later stages of development as well. He started by considering the crucially important role of the father in the child's emotional development. Once again, we must acknowledge that his thinking was developed at a time where societal expectations were of a family unit comprising of traditional family roles. In today's society, families have evolved to encompass a wider range of units and which may be captured by the term "partner of the primary carer". However, for the sake of simplicity regarding the fundamentals of Winnicott's ideas the term father will be referred to.

Winnicott felt that the father's role may be dependent on what the mother will allow, but stated very strongly the father's involvement is important from the earliest stages of the child's life. He felt that the main function, in the early stages of complete dependence was to support the mother in her state of maternal preoccupation, thereby enabling the mother and child to engage, undisturbed, by outside pressures, in the enmeshed relationship where the mother is able to tolerate and meet the child's high dependence needs.

Winnicott described the next function of the father to be the recipient of negative feelings from the child. This very much overlaps the work of Melanie Klein (1945, 1946), who will be considered in a later chapter. Most analytic thinking would agree that in the early stages of life, the child is a mass of primitive feelings, some positive and some negative. For example positive feelings of being fed and then outraged anger when the breast does not arrive. The ability in the child to tolerate ambivalent feelings towards the primary carer comes at a later stage of development, around two to three in a child without disabilities. Prior to this, the child needs to give the negative feelings to Dad because they are not yet ready to tolerate ambivalent feelings towards the mother who, at this stage of life, is the most loved person. The third role of the father Winnicott felt was to provide fun and stimulation to the child and confirmation of sense of self as a valued person.

Winnicott also outlined the impact of absent fathers, which he had a lot of experience of working with children at the time of World War II when many fathers were away fighting. This thinking is particularly important when thinking about children with disabilities in the fact that the relationship breakdown rate amongst families with a child with disabilities is much higher than the already high divorce rate. Winnicott described how children may idealise absent fathers and they become a source of fantasy, often thought to be better than they are. A child kept away from his father will be confused and have a way of labelling things or of struggling to label things that can create a great deal of tension in him. Winnicott felt that if a small baby is left with only one recipient for his positive and negative feelings then the child will become very confused. In other words, he needs to have a depository for positive and negative feelings that is separate for each until the tolerance of good and bad in the same person is achieved.

Winnicott expands quite a lot on small children and their fantasies about sex and the parental relationship, stressing that children have their own ideas that may be very different to ours. *The Piggle* (1971b) is a book he wrote describing a therapy around these issues. This issue becomes relevant when thinking about a person with learning disabilities, because at the core of their self-belief may be that they were made from "bad sex". Hollins and Sinason (2000) describe this as being one of the "three secrets" carried by people with learning disabilities. Winnicott also described the possibility of a belief that one of the parents is not their parent, as a sort of wishful thinking.

In talking about families, Winnicott also described the experience of very young parents who had recently left their own parents. This was very much a factor of society at the time he was writing, where it was much more common for young people to enter into marriage and set up homes of their own as a way of leaving the parental home. His reflections still have resonance with the experience of very young parents today, some of who may openly say that they want a child to have someone to love who will love and need them, but are not emotionally prepared for the level of dependence and the demands the baby will make on them. For young parents with a child with disabilities this issue may be compounded and add to the other pressures on young parents. Again, this highlights the need for identification and understanding of this issue and the support it demands.

Winnicott stressed the need in a family for each person to have space in their lives where they are able to be in charge and make choices, that everyone should have some part of their life over which they are king or queen, including small children. This area may be their room or the clothes they wear. Obviously, the parents need to be the ones in charge, in a healthy development, but in cases where this becomes so dominant that the child has no control over any part of their life at all, this may cause detrimental difficulties to the emotional development of the child. For a child with a disability there may be much less chance of them being able to do this because someone does it for them or because they do it wrong. They literally may not have the volition or power in the family to do the things they want to do.

Winnicott described the transitional object, more commonly known as a security blanket or toy. As the child becomes older, the object, whether a ragged piece of cloth or a toy, represents the feelings of safety and security of the relationship with his mother. Having the transitional object whilst away from the mother allows the child to bear the anxiety of being separated from his primary carer. In a child with disabilities, whose cries may be inconsistent, whose ability to reach out, hold on, or point may be severely impaired, the parent's opportunities to identify the significance of the object to the child may be much reduced. The child therefore does not have the same chance in their development to have the object that gives them that feeling of safety and security (ego strengthening) when away from the parents.

Transitional objects can be seen to be an issue in some adults with learning disabilities. The person may not have been able to develop beyond the stage where this object is needed and so be seen in adulthood to have what can be sometimes termed obsessional attachment to the object, their desire for the object deemed as not age appropriate. If the emotional significance and need for this object is acknowledged, then ways can be found so as not to stigmatise the person, for example a doll can be carried in a bag when out. Additionally, clinical work can involve the teaching of a person to have a transitional object such as a photograph of somebody loved or an item of clothing or other objects. This can provide much comfort and a sense of security and especially so at times of stress.

Another role that Winnicott talked about for the family was to tolerate the backwards and forwards process of emotional growth in the child. By this, he meant that children, from the age of birth to five go through a huge amount of emotional development. However, naturally, sometimes this will slip back and they will seem to lose some of their maturity. Winnicott felt this needs to be tolerated by parents, rather than being chastised, and accepted as part of the process of development. In children with learning disabilities, signs of progress may be very much wished and hoped for, so the natural slipping back may be felt more keenly by the parents as this may be loaded with wishes and expectations. Helping parents to understand that this is a natural part of any child's development may help them to manage this process. Additionally due to the reasons discussed earlier, the child may be dependent for much longer emotionally, and parents will need to understand that this dependence is needed before independence can be developed.

Good enough parenting

The importance of good enough parenting and its necessary failures was discussed earlier. In the older child, intelligence and the development of rationalisation enables the child to learn to cope when things do not go perfectly. A child who believes that everyone knew that when he wanted a drink it had to be orange, but one day was given blackcurrant, if they are able to rationalise, rather than becoming very distressed would label the experience as "that person doesn't know any better" or "there's no orange left". By being able to label and understand the experience it makes it okay instead of a source of distress.

This ability to rationalise does require intelligence, the ability to handle more than one thought at the same time. The child with cognitive impairment is likely to have more difficulty in developing the skills of rationalisation. This difficulty may be further compounded because of more limited opportunities to experience the world, which limits the number of concepts the child has.

The home

Winnicott stressed that the child takes in information not only from his parents, or the people that are there to offer consistent, reliable care, but also his family home. The family home contributes to the feeling of safety and security that children need to be able to emotionally develop. He found through his work during World War II, children whose homes had been destroyed, sometimes fearing that they were the cause of the tragedy. In my own clinical experience, I have found that children who moved home before the age of five, often have concern, fear, and a lack of understanding about what made the house disappear. It is as though they cannot keep the house in mind, cannot rationalise, so it feels like it has been taken away.

This is very important to think about with adults with learning disabilities who may have challenging behaviour and be destructive to their environment, including their homes. It is important, in helping someone to emotionally develop that the physical consistency of this home is maintained as much as possible and therefore repairs made when damage has occurred.

It also needs to be acknowledged that adults over forty may have experienced time living in an institution. Prior to institutional closures, in the 1970s onwards it was a tragically common experience that a child with disabilities would leave the family home to live in an institution, partly due to the beliefs that were around at the time about service provision. Sometimes children were sent to institutions because of challenging behaviour. For whatever reason it occurred, it meant the loss for the child, not only of the relationship with the caregivers, but also of the secure home base. A child with learning disabilities would have had less ability to understand and rationalise what was happening.

Use in trauma-informed care

So far, there has been an examination of the key elements needed in a healthy emotional development and the factors that can impact on this in a child with learning disabilities. Some of the likely consequences in later life have been explored. It is very common to find that a person without disabilities presenting with mental health problems later in life has had some failure in this early experience. For people with learning disabilities presenting distressed or challenging behaviour in adulthood, there is an increased chance, because of their disability that they will have experienced some failure in this early emotional development. This may be due to features of the disability impacting on the process or the additional stressors impacting on the parent's ability to deliver good enough care.

An example would be the person who has been acting out the consequences of a disruption in receiving good enough care which has left them with lifelong issues. These difficulties can compound the disability they already have. The beliefs of those supporting the person, if not including an understanding of emotional failures can further complicate the situation leading to management strategies that can compound the persons difficulties further.

In the TIC model, by understanding the implications of these failures, interventions can be directed at meeting the person's emotional needs, of giving them an experience of good enough care that incorporates the elements of what has been missed, and the consequent trauma.

In therapy, these needs are met by the therapy providing an emotionally "holding" environment where the therapist is reliable, consistent, and nurturing in their meetings and interactions with the person. The therapist will be able to accept the person as they are, including their dependence. The therapeutic work will, at some level, include a processing of the extreme emotions the person is experiencing. Through this, the person may then be able to have a good flow of emotion from the inside to the outside and back again.

This acceptance of dependence can be provided through therapy and or an emotionally nurturing environment, which will be discussed further in later chapters. These can provide the building blocks on which a person can begin to develop a more robust sense of self or personality that has not been possible before.

CHAPTER TWO

Bowlby

In this chapter, we will explore the work of John Bowlby on attachment and relate this to people with learning disabilities. He was a paediatrician and psychoanalyst who worked in the 1960s and 1970s and was a colleague of Winnicott's. He was the first person to notice the behaviours in children which he labelled as attachment behaviours and his work has been very influential in informing child care policy since the 1960s. Others have written about attachment but all follow from Bowlby's original ideas. He wrote a number of books on this topic which have now been printed together in a book called *A Secure Base* (1979).

Bowlby wrote that human beings have a natural tendency or "drive" to make affectional bonds with other people. Here the word bond means a close and intimate connection with another person. Making affectional bonds is the basic foundation of human social and emotional life. It is a common belief that babies do not begin to form attachments until they are about one year old. However, Bowlby found that a newborn baby will begin to make proximal bonds, that is, bond to those nearest him from birth, but the signs of attachment behaviour are not seen until the second half of the first year. By this stage, the child should be showing signs of preference for who is there for him, the person who makes him feel safe.

If this person is absent then signs of distress will be evident, indicating that the person is the attachment figure. Children first protest, but then freeze and become uninvolved with their surroundings, only returning to normal behaviour when the attachment figure returns. Bowlby noticed that the child will go through a number of distinct stages. Initially he will protest very loudly, demanding to know where the person is. The child then moves into the next stage of despair where he becomes very distressed, screams, cries, and will not be able to be comforted by others. If the attachment figure has not returned after some time, the child will then move into a state where he appears not to notice the person is missing or that it doesn't matter. In the past, this was interpreted as the child being at ease with the separation. However, Bowlby found that the child was actually moving into a stage of mourning or depression at the loss of the attachment figure. At this stage, in the child's mind, he has "given up" and has accepted the fact that he's been abandoned. When the attachment figure returns, the child initially feels insecure and is unsure whether or not he will be abandoned again. However, if the child is securely attached, this will soon pass and the child will be relatively easy to comfort and will show joy at the person returning. It is important that the child is helped to process the feelings about the separation and is reassured.

Bowlby was instrumental in changing the way that children are supported in hospital from one of denying parental visits to the free access that is provided today. In the past, it was thought that children, who went quiet after the initial protest, had adapted, but Bowlby recognised that they had, in fact, gone into a state of mourning. This inevitably hindered their prospects of recovery as well. It is strange for us now to realise that this is only fifty years ago that we realised the emotional damage that can be done when access to the secure emotional base is denied.

Once the bond has been made it will stay solid and strong and last for a lifetime. The first bonds that a child makes are called the primary attachments. These attachments are vital for the survival of the baby who needs the parent to nurture and care for it. Bowlby stressed that children do develop secondary attachments and will cope for periods of time with another person, so long as they are clearly approved of by the primary attachment figure. This can be seen most frequently with relationships with grandparents, who are present from time to time, remain reliable, and are clearly accepted by the mother. The more time an adult spends with a child and the more the needs are met, the stronger the attachment will be.

These strong primary attachments are the building blocks for good emotional health in later life, as they enable the individual to make healthy relationship bonds with others. Disturbances in this process can lead to difficulties relating to others and in forming relationships which can contribute to emotional and psychological difficulties.

For the child to make an attachment, the primary carer needs to be available and present. They need to be consistent, reliable, positive, and encouraging in their relationship with the child to enable it to feel safe and secure in his primary attachment. It is the quality of the emotional relationship that is important, not what the child is given in terms of the material trappings of family life. This secure attachment helps the child to develop a robust sense of self and of being good enough and enables the child to relate to other people and form healthy relationships later in life. About sixty per cent of children are able to make this kind of attachment.

Once the primary attachment has been made, this relationship becomes what Bowlby called the secure base, or safe base. This is not referring to a location but rather the actual relationship where the child feels safe and secure. The child feels safe enough to explore the world, knowing that it has the relationship to return to. This idea is very similar to what Winnicott said about the good enough mother helping the child to feel secure enough to explore the world.

Developing independence

Bowlby said that "the aim of attachment was to detach", meaning that if the child has a strong affectional bond with his primary care giver, he will, when growing up, separate and become independent and then be able to attach to other people in adult life such as friends, partner and children. It is not possible for the child to be independent and separate, in a healthy way, as an adult if he has not first been attached and then detached from the primary care giver.

A good, strong, secure attachment will enable the child to make good, strong attachments throughout the rest of their lives. He will be self-reliant and have the self-confidence to think, "I'm all right, I'm an okay person, and I'm able to live an okay life". He will be able to work and collaborate with others and make a good team player, as he is self-confident and self-reliant enough not to be threatened in a group situation; he is able to "give and take". He has a personality that is interdependent, meaning that he is neither over dependent on others nor too independent.

When things go wrong

Difficulties with attachments in early life can affect emotional and psychological functioning in later life, leading many people to need some form of therapeutic input. How this can happen will now be explored further and then there will be consideration of how people with learning disabilities may be even more vulnerable to experiencing these difficulties.

An insecure attachment

If the child does not receive enough reliable, consistent care for a bond to develop, his attachment will be insecure or not formed at all. He does not have a safe base from which to explore and enter into the wider world. A child who is insecurely attached will react differently to separation. He will go to anyone who is available, he doesn't recognise that it is only some people who provide the safe base and security and that other people don't. Consequently, he may be very vulnerable. Such children may also seem very clingy, as if they are trying to hang on to the person they are with. They will not be as self-confident as a securely attached child and won't have a robust sense of being okay or good enough. They often find it hard to give and take in relationships. In adulthood, these people may find it difficult to attach to other people and their relationships may either be very superficial or be very possessive due to not being able to give and take.

Permanent separation

Bowlby identified that the period from fifteen to thirty months of age is the most crucial time for maintaining the consistent presence of the attachment figure to allow strong, secure attachments to build. This is the stage the child is beginning to explore the world as he can walk and he needs the secure base to go back to. If this is not there, the child will stop exploring the world, may become depressed and stop engaging with other people.

We have already looked at the stages a child goes through when he is separated from his primary attachment figure. However, if at this crucial age the separation lasts longer than six months, happens repeatedly, or is permanent due to a tragedy, then the child enters a stage of pathological mourning. Without appropriate help and support the child won't be able to attach to other people and there is a danger of him becoming permanently detached and he may not ever recover from this enough to be able to make further attachments in later life.

This state of permanent detachment or pathological mourning can often be seen in adults if they experienced serious separations in childhood or were taken into care. In this state, people just accept the loss, without the mixed emotions of anger, despair, and sadness that usually accompany such a loss. These emotions are instead often deeply repressed. They may find it very difficult to engage in relationships and there is often an absence of love and friendship. They may be given a diagnosis of "depression" or "borderline personality disorder", but what is actually happening is a permanent state of mourning for the "lost self", or the person they would have been if the affectional bond had not been broken too soon.

Pathological parenting

Bowlby coined the term "pathological parenting" to describe how someone may be affected even if the primary care givers have been available, but the nature of this care has harmed the child. This can happen in many different ways such as the parents may have been consistently unresponsive, rejecting, or negative to the child. The child is left with a sense of "what's wrong with me?" He is not able to rationalise or understand why the parent is being the way they are. The small child will internalise how the parent is with him and will not grow up seeing himself as a good enough person. If the attachment figure comes and goes, either through illness or for other reasons, the child is left in a state of not knowing whether the carer is going to be reliable or not, affecting his sense of security. The child will wonder if the parent is going to be there in the morning or the next week. This will have a huge impact on the child's ability to be secure in his attachments and therefore the child's ability to grow and develop. Sometimes an exasperated parent may make threats such as "I won't love you any more" in an attempt to discipline a child. However if the child hears this often, they are unable to know whether the parent means it or not, leaving them with a sense of being unlovable. This sense can be taken into adulthood and affect future wellbeing. Continual threats that are conditional, for example "I'll only love you if you're good" or "I'll only love you if you're clean", can lead to the child and later the adult, desperately trying to be good enough to be loved, leading to distorted or obsessive behaviours, for example, excessive cleaning.

It is not uncommon to hear a parent saying to a small child, "If you don't behave, I will leave you here", or "If you don't come now, I'm going", in an attempt to try and get a child to comply. Most parents don't mean it; however, some do and will actually leave the child. This threat of being abandoned, if it occurs regularly, or is carried out, is more than a little child can take psychologically. As a consequence he may become very clingy or run around after people. In later life he may be very dependent on others or be very fearful of being abandoned and left alone. Sometimes as adults, people stay in unhealthy or damaging relationships because they cannot bear to be alone. Sometimes struggling parents may say things such as "You'll be the death of me", "Looking after you is killing me", or even "I'm going to kill you". A young child is unable to rationalise these comments, to think about what is going on for the parent to make them say it. Hearing such comments frequently can again have a detrimental effect on the child's sense of self and their development. Similarly, statements that blame the child and make him feel guilty such as "You've driven me to this", "You've made me ill", put enormous pressure on a young child to the detriment of his emotional development.

So far, we have examined the impact of disrupted and pathological attachments on the child, which can affect his sense of self and the person he becomes later in life. It can also affect his future relationships, both friendships and intimate relationships and can also have an impact on the relationship with his own children. Children may be left going through life carrying a feeling that they are not good enough, not loveable or with immense guilt. The tragedy of this is that they were good enough and lovable to start with, but it is the parenting they have received that has left them with these difficulties. It is thought about

Have to provide love to Peter Lee all times.

forty per cent of children have an insecure attachment. Most of these do not reach the criteria for accessing outside support from services. Of this group with insecure attachments, in severe situations, will be people with a diagnosis of borderline personality disorder, dissociative disorders, and, in really severe cases, psychopathy.

In extreme cases, people who experience disorganised attachment in early childhood develop personality difficulties. Disorganised attachment is the condition where the figure who should be providing the safe base, does so in a negative and damaging way, usually with cruelty and inconsistency. The child can only keep the attachment figure if he complies with activities that are abusive and often painful. The consequent confusion results in the splitting off parts of the mind into other selves. At its worst, this becomes Dissociative Identity Disorder (previously known as Multiple Personality Disorder), where more than one defined personality develops. One self-state or personality is active in some circumstances and another at other times. People who go into adulthood from this position are usually extremely distressed and may be labelled seriously mentally ill. Their treatment is long and requires the establishment of another primary attachment figure that it stronger and more consistent than the one who did the damage.

Children with disabilities

A child with learning disability may be vulnerable in many ways to having their ability to form attachments disrupted, due to the disability. The child may have frequent separations from the primary care giver due to respite care or stays in hospital and may not get enough consistent time with the parent to be able to make an attachment. The very disability itself, especially if it is physical, may affect the child's ability to stay in close proximity and chase after the parent or follow them if they leave the room. From the parents' point of view this may be a relief as they do not have to be so vigilant of the child's whereabouts, but it can have a lasting impact on the child's ability to attach to the primary carer. Also, a physical disability that affects mobility may affect the child's ability to explore the world from the safe base.

Becoming a parent is a massive change in any person's life. It can at times feel extremely stressful and overwhelming. Having a child with disabilities can increase this stress and worry. Additionally the parents may be grieving for the "perfect child" they thought they would have and can struggle to come to terms with the disability. In these circumstances, it can be hard for parents just to keep going. Under this stress, parents may end up resorting to saying things that they don't mean, the types of things that Bowlby described as "pathological parenting". If the child has learning disabilities, he will have even less understanding of why the parent is saying these things or be less likely to be able to rationalise the situation. This will lead to him being in an even more insecure position with potential interference in the development of the sense of self.

Children with disabilities who present with emotional and behavioural difficulties in later life often have disorganised attachments and may also have experienced cruelty. However, it is more common to find that they have had multiple carers because of their disability, through respite care or residential school, and this is what has disturbed their attachments and consequent sense of self. People over forty may have spent some period of their younger life in an institution, away from their families altogether as this was the most common type of care provision at the time.

The most disturbed people we find in adult services have either had no clear attachment figure and have never had the opportunity to develop close relationships with anyone, or they have experienced cruelty in their primary relationships and have not been able to make sense of this. The development of the ability to rationalise, to think and evaluate what is happening to you, will be impaired in people with intellectual disabilities. Consequently, they are more at risk of psychological breakdown when the world does not make sense. Disorganised attachments clearly fall into the category of a world that does not make sense.

Even if a person has been able to have good attachments in childhood, the very experience of being disabled in our society will lessen the opportunities for relationships to be made throughout life. Bowlby felt that in adult life we need attachments with between six and ten people for optimum mental health. As anyone undertaking "getting to know you" work with someone with learning disabilities the number of good attachment relationships someone has in their life may be a lot less than this, or those that do exist are made of people who are paid to be in the person's life such as carers or other professionals.

Implications for Bowlby's ideas on the Frankish model

If we can acknowledge the emotional pain and disruption that comes from disrupted attachments then interventions can be put into place to help address some of these issues. For those people receiving residential support, Bowlby's ideas help us to realise how important it is for an individual to feel safe and secure with the people supporting them. Often in services, there is a fear of a person making an attachment to their carers and it may be positively discouraged. However, if we can accept that a basic human need is to feel safe and secure in our relationships and that for people being provided with care, the carers are usually the main source of relationships, then a different way of thinking about this can develop. By ensuring that a person has a consistent, reliable staff team around them we can begin to establish a sense of security or safe base for the person. Drawing from a group of five or six staff means the person will always be supported by people they are familiar with, even in holidays, sick leave or if a staff member leaves.

A named worker system, whereby the person is designated a staff member and knows who is going to be there for them for the day, is going to engender more of a sense of security than being told "there are two staff on today". The named worker does not have to spend the whole time with the person, but rather keep the person informed of their whereabouts, so that the person knows where to find them if they need them. With this provision, the person will develop attachments to these staff and it is through these attachments that he can begin to develop and grow as a person.

Obviously staff will not be able to be with the person forever, but as long as this is not promised to the person, rather that the person knows that staff care about them and can be trusted, they should be able to develop enough ego strength to cope when a staff member leaves, especially when they have other familiar staff in their group available to support them. Indeed, it is a very common human experience to have relationships where a bond or attachment is formed, which may end for any number of reasons. To have this experience is part of life and by "protecting" people from this loss, we are preventing any chance they have of being able to experience the security needed for emotional growth.

It is interesting to note that some of the prescribed behavioural treatments for people with autism are based on the ideas of the secure base. By maintaining sameness—for example, colour coding domestic equipment in programmes—is a way of saying the world can be safe. Similarly, the provision of one-to-one staff allocation is recognising the need for the security of a person. It is often seen as a supervisory need but observation of individuals reveals that it is the certainty that someone is there that makes the difference, not the perceived threat of sanctions if behaviour deteriorates. It is fascinating that a lot of effort is put into programming complex interventions, when the answer and the intervention that works, is in fact very simple. It is almost certainly a need in the providers of the intervention to intellectualise the response to the distress as a defence against the pain of recognising the emotional pain that is evident in unattached people.

People with attachment difficulties may be incredibly difficult to work with at times. They may be extremely needy at times and very rejecting at others. They may display extreme sadness. Staff working with such individuals will need support to enable them to deal with the emotional fallout of working so intensively with such people. Staff themselves may have experienced difficulties in their own childhood and this support can help them to unravel the delicate interplay in their relationship history with the people they support.

In some cases, a person may need more intensive therapeutic support to help him overcome his attachment issues. Therapy is not about blaming others; it is about helping a person to understand what has happened to them and the patterns of behaviour they have developed to survive, which are now maladaptive in adulthood. Gaining these insights can help a person to choose a different way of relating. Prior to this point of gaining insight, the therapy will provide the person with the safe base and attachment (to the therapist) that they have been previously lacking. For a while, the therapist may become the most important person in the person's life. However the experience of a consistent, positive, nurturing relationship will help the person develop the ego strength to be able to gain insights into their life. The boundaried requirements of therapy, that is, same time, day, and place, will increase the chances of the person experiencing this relationship as consistent and reliable. There may be a need for the therapist to undertake some educative work with the system around the individual to help them understand the process and also tackle any difficult emotions that may arise from the therapist becoming the most important person to the client during the process of therapy.

Therapy may need to be very long term, although the availability of this is very dependent of local resources. However, such long term work which may go on for several years, will be extremely beneficial for the person in that they will be able to develop enough of a sense of self and agency to be able to manage their own feelings and relationships enough and to be able to manage with reduced incidents of distressed behaviour.

CHAPTER THREE

Margaret Mahler

The theoretical ideas of Winnicott and Bowlby considered so far give a good basis for understanding early emotional development. They show us the ingredients needed for "optimum" emotional development and also the mechanisms and possible consequences when things go wrong. Their work, however, does not give us the ability to measure the stage of development that a child has reached, or to identify if progress is made to a further stage.

Margaret Mahler helps us in these two areas. Her seminal text, *The Psychological Birth of the Human Infant*, (1979) has been one of the most significant influences in the development of the trauma-informed care model. Mahler, working in America with a team of researchers, used a specially designed nursery with observation mirrors to observe young children up to the age of five with their primary carers, throughout their early years of emotional development in a natural environment.

Through this work, they were able to identify the stages, or what Mahler termed "phases", (the terms are used interchangeably) of emotional development that a child goes through from the physical birth to the psychological birth or, as Mahler termed it, "individuation". This is the point in emotional development at which the child has "hatched" the beginnings of his own personality and self-identity, and has developed his ability to relate to and interact with others in the world around.

Perhaps most importantly for our current consideration is that they were also able to identify the behavioural characteristics that can be seen, and therefore measured, at each of the stages in the children's emotional development. Mahler and her colleagues were also able to identify the role of the parent, or attachment figure, in facilitating the child's emotional development. From this work, Mahler supported the work of previous theorists; that emotional development cannot happen in isolation and that for it to occur it is essential that the child is part of a two-way relationship in which the child has an attachment to the other person, be that the parent or other attachment figure.

For me, Mahler's work proved to be fundamental to the development of the trauma-informed care model. Mahler's work helped me to develop a method for measuring emotional development, therefore being more scientific and integrating her psychology and psychotherapy practice. I found the descriptions of the behaviours present in the different stages of emotional development resonated with what I had seen among the people with learning disabilities I had been around earlier in my life and also those I have worked with during my career. I developed this insight to argue that for some people with learning disabilities, because of their vulnerability to compromised early emotional development experiences, which can occur due to their very disability, they can become "stuck" or arrested at a stage of emotional development. If appropriate support is not given, the person can stay stuck at this stage throughout their life and furthermore the behaviours that the person shows, which correspond to their stage of emotional development, if not understood, may be seen as problematic or challenging.

In this chapter, there will be an overview of Mahler's stages. This will be followed by a consideration of how these ideas can be utilised to assess the emotional development stages of people with learning disabilities.

Margaret Mahler's phases of emotional development

Mahler refers to six phases or stages which are described below, but generally, only four are considered within the Frankish model.

Symbiotic phase. This phase relates to the earliest stage of human development where the newborn child appears to be still connected to his parent. If you observe a mother with a newborn there is no emotional space between them, they are enmeshed, entirely interdependent. In other words, they are "symbiotic" and there is no room for anyone else in the relationship at this very early stage.

In typical development this stage lasts only a short time, usually the first few weeks of life, and therefore is very rarely seen other than in this naturally occurring situation. It is extremely rare to see an adult who is still in the symbiotic phase, although Frankish did see one adult who was still in the symbiotic relationship with his mother in his early forties. There was some suggestion that he may have regressed because he had been in bed since he was nineteen, when he had an illness and never got up again. At the time of working with him, he had only nightclothes, was fed in bed, and washed by his mother like a baby. He was referred because he had become too demanding of her, as she got older. It is exceptionally rare to find people at this stage and it is, therefore, not usually considered in the TIC model.

Differentiation phase. After the first few weeks of life, the baby begins to develop an awareness of existing separate from the mother. The baby has begun to move into the differentiation phase, as he is learning to differentiate himself from the mother and the world around him. During this phase the baby becomes aware of himself, parts of his own body, and his immediate surroundings. The baby begins to look at his hands and feet, perhaps play with his genitals, and to look at things that come into his field of vision. The baby will look at the sides of the cot and toys that are put within easy reach. He will react to an adult who comes into visual contact, but does not appear to retain the visual image once the person has gone out of range.

The presence and availability of the parent or attachment figure is a vital part of the child making progress through the differentiation phase. The communications of the baby at this stage are all "self-referenced", meaning that they are about the child having a need, such as being hungry or cold, or in pain. A vital part of the carer's role, in helping the baby progress through this stage, is to identify and meet his needs. By the carer doing this, the child is learning about the first rudimentary basics of human relationships and interaction as well as having a good enough care experience. Additionally the parents need to be able to facilitate the baby's increasing need to explore his environment and the world around him.

Mahler identified the behaviours that are observable at this stage as being the personal exploratory behaviours of looking at and touching oneself, and the reaction to the sight of a significant other. This phase lasts until about seven or eight months and as the child progresses through it, the exploratory behaviours gradually expand from exploring just the immediate environment to taking an interest in the wider environment and exploring through other sensory modalities such as mouthing objects. This development corresponds with the child's physical and visual development.

It must be noted that we all engage in some differentiation behaviours, for example, twiddling hair or earrings, scratching, and hiding under the duvet when stressed. They are behaviours that do not need another person and provide some relief from anxiety for the individual.

Practising phase. At about seven or eight months there is rapid neurological expansion of the brain, which involves the development of skills in the baby and corresponds with the practising stage. Neurological connections are made and the child becomes able to do a new behaviour, such as dropping or throwing toys, moving about, sitting up, or making noises. What Mahler observed was that when the child became able to do something new, he would repeat or practise that new skill over and over again until he became proficient, strengthening the neurological connection, or until further neurological development meant that another skill became available to him. Children at this stage can be seen repetitively throwing a rattle or building a brick castle and knocking it down over and over just for the pure joy of being able to do it.

In terms of the role of the parent or attachment figure in helping the child to progress through this stage, responding to their self-referenced communications and behaviours continues to be crucial. Additionally Mahler observed that the practising behaviours were more frequent and carried out with more enthusiasm by the child in the presence of the attachment figure. The practising behaviours may happen when the child is alone but Mahler noted that the level of activity is much reduced. The implication is that at this stage there is the beginning of the recognition that someone else is paying attention, and that the attention is welcomed. As this is an essential part of human interaction, it is clear that this is yet another building block on the road to meaningful two-person communication. Therefore, the presence and attention of the attachment figure when practising behaviours are being undertaken is extremely important in enabling the child to progress through this stage. In terms of attachment behaviour, it has long been recognised that children stop engaging in play if their significant other disappears. This is clearly a similar phenomenon to what Mahler describes in talking about the practising stage.

Practising behaviours are seen very clearly in people with autism. They persist in all of us to some extent, in that we will practise a new skill when we choose to, but this is qualitatively slightly different as it has a bigger element of purposefulness. In early childhood, the purpose is to become proficient in a skill that has just been discovered through development. As adults, there is more of a cognitive element. We do all, however, have some habits from childhood that belong to this group of behaviours.

Early rapprochement. The move on to more meaningful two-way interaction happens with the beginning of the early rapprochement phase which starts around the age of fifteen months, but can of course vary from child to child. Early rapprochement is about the development of give-and-take, of two-way interaction and negotiation in relationships. It is about the forming of more mature relationship skills that will be used throughout life.

During this phase, there is rapid development of motor and vocal skills. One of the first signs of early rapprochement is the child's ability to say "no" or to walk away. This development of language is the first step in negotiation, in expressing personal wishes and resistance. Similarly, with walking, as the child becomes able to run away, the relationship between the attachment figure and the child is changed.

Sometimes the child who learns to walk early will find that they are physically able to walk away from the significant other, before being emotionally able to cope with that separation. In these children, it is possible to observe the anxiety that is created by the unexpected distance between themselves and the primary carer. The ability of the parent to facilitate the growing independence of the child, while keeping the world safe at the same time, will have a significant impact on the child's positive progress through the early rapprochement stage. The parent or attachment figure will, of course, be the person with whom the child practises and develops his negotiation and two-way communication skills and the parent needs to be able to be tolerant and encouraging of this process, as this is crucially important in the child's development of relationship skills as well of his sense of himself in the world.

Parents or other significant others have a great deal of responsibility in ensuring that all goes well in this stage. However, the ability of the child to develop and use these skills will also influence what is essentially a two-way process between himself and his carers. The early rapprochement phase can be lots of fun, and exciting, in that the development is rapid and the personality of the child begins to show through. Children who have happily progressed through the differentiation and practising stages, with no hiccups and no anxiety, will enter into early rapprochement with excitement and enthusiasm. They will have the joy of learning within the security of the relationship with the significant other, and the certainty that they are valued and respected. Children who have had difficulties in the earlier stages may enter early rapprochement in a less adventurous and excited way. If they have not been secure in their relationship with their primary carer, the risk of exploring the world away from the primary carer will be more daunting.

Mahler's research showed that the behaviours seen at this stage are two-way interactions that may be initiated by either party. Also, there are obvious signs that the child is taking note of the impact of his behaviour on other people as well as taking note of the impact of other people's behaviour on himself. So, for example, the child may look as though he is going to drop food on the floor and will watch for the parental reaction. Similarly, the parent may put on a coat and the child will watch to see what this means to him. This is qualitatively different from the practising stage, where the presence of the other person is appreciated but is not vital.

Separation in the early rapprochement stage can be traumatic, as the child has become very dependent on the reliability of the significant other to be consistent in their reactions. The child at this stage who has to suddenly access a different significant other will need to relearn his way of relating, which will create anxiety, and will impair development.

Early rapprochement behaviours are the ones seen most frequently in people with disabilities and challenging behaviour. It is as if they are constantly trying to work out the rules of engagement.

Late rapprochement. The stage of late rapprochement covers the period from about age two until around three or three-and-a-half years. Mahler found that the end of the late rapprochement phase is marked by some sort of "rapprochement crisis", which marks the point the child gains acceptance of psychological separation from the significant other. This is what Mahler termed the "psychological birth" where the child has progressed through the stages of development and formed what will be the backbone of his personality for the rest of life. Obviously the young child at this stage will still be dependent on the parents for psychological support for many years to come, but it is at this point the child is now psychologically separate and has become his own person who will continue to grow and develop separately from the parents.

The late rapprochement phase involves the child gradually increasing his level of independence, within the context of the secure relationship he has with the parent or attachment figure. He is not only increasingly exploring the world but also his place in the world, including his relationships. This stage can be very testing for the child's carers, both in terms of needing to keep the child physically safe, but also in being able to tolerate the increasingly demanding "pushing of the boundaries" as the child tests out his place in the world.

The parent who holds back or restricts this growing independence risks the child becoming anxious and becoming an anxious adult. This is because this is the phase of developing confidence through increasing exploration of the world and increasing distance from the parent, or safe base, as Bowlby would term it but with the safe relationship to return to for security. A child who is thwarted at this stage is not able to develop this confidence and does not experience gradual risk taking with the safety net of the parental relationship to return to.

Mahler found that the observable behaviours indicating that the child is in the late rapprochement stage are notably negotiation behaviours, often seen as arguing and tantrums. Also observable is the child's ability to play at increasing distances from the attachment figure, but needing to know they are there for what Bowlby termed "emotional refuelling". Mahler also observed the child asking for things and responding to when being spoken to or interacted with.

Individuation: The sixth, and final, phase of emotional development that Mahler described was that of individuation. As previously mentioned, this follows the rapprochement crisis, that point at which the child realises that he is separate. The anxiety is either accepted calmly, or there is a big tantrum that ends with acceptance that the anxiety has to be managed. Individuation is the development of the sense of self, the personality that the child will take forward into adulthood. The rapprochement crisis may be visible in the form of a tantrum, but may be less obvious in the form of a quiet acceptance of separation from the significant other. In terms of the TIC model, it follows that we are rarely asked to intervene and help people who have successfully individuated, as they have a formed sense of self that can negotiate for needs to be met. Consequently, we need to pay little attention to individuation for the purposes of understanding the TIC model. It is perhaps necessary to mention that people can regress from being individuated if they experience trauma in later life, and will possibly need therapy to address this. If they have been successfully individuated before the traumatic event, they will usually recover their equilibrium quite quickly.

Summary of Margaret Mahler's stages

Margaret Mahler researched the behaviour of children within the parent–child dyad. From her observations, she was able to identify particular behaviours that were real and relevant to different stages of emotional development. She was also able to identify the factors that were vital to the successful progress through each of the stages. The essential ingredient throughout the stages from symbiosis to individuation was the availability of a reliable and consistent significant other. This clearly agrees with Winnicott and Bowlby. What she adds to their work is the description of the behaviours that can be observed.

When things go wrong

Mahler's work showed very clearly that the emotional development of the child is very much dependent on the two-way relationship between the child and his attachment figure. It is a complex process based on the delicate interplay of interaction and reciprocation between the child and his parent.

If this input from the attachment figure is not available, which can occur for a whole array of reasons, babies will withdraw into themselves and not acquire the first building blocks in the development of human relationships. This has been shown to some extent in animal studies many years ago, and was also evident in the orphans who were found in Romania. Babies left with no human contact in those very early stages have a blank look in their eyes, and cannot make sense of human contact.

The parent who is neglectful during these critical stages will be laying down the foundations for a depressed adult; and the parent who is cruel or abusive will be laying down the potential for serious mental illness or personality disorder.

How this relates to people with learning disabilities

We have already seen in earlier chapters how the early life experiences of children with learning disabilities are more vulnerable to disturbance. The emphasis in the findings of the work of Margaret Mahler is that the emotional development of the child is very delicately balanced on the interactions between the child and his parent. The learning-disabled child can be seen to be more vulnerable to disruptions in this process. The possible psychological and emotional impact upon the parents of having a child with learning disabilities as well as the increased likelihood of separations between the parent and child due to hospital stays, or respite placements, all increase the likelihood of some disturbance in this delicately balanced process. Added to this is the fact that the child himself, because of his disability, may not be able to be as active in seeking the interaction needed for his development. This can add to the vulnerability of the process being affected as well. This means that a child with learning disabilities is more vulnerable to having his progress through the stages of emotional development impeded. He is likely to take longer to progress through than the three and a half years found by Mahler. I reported how a child can become "stuck" at a stage of emotional development and if he is not given the appropriate input may stay "arrested" at that stage of emotional development throughout life (1989).

What happens if development is arrested

As previously mentioned it is exceptionally rare to find someone stuck at the symbiosis phase of emotional development so that won't be considered here.

Someone stuck at the differentiation stage of emotional development appears to be stuck "in their own world". They may appear only interested in their immediate environment or their bodies. They may pick at their clothing or twirl their hair. Much of their exhibited behaviour is self-stimulatory. They may call out to other people around them but this will be to get a need met, that is, needing a drink or needing the toilet, in other words it will be a self-referenced behaviour. They may watch around them but seem passive and not to appear to be interested in taking part unless it is to get the attention of someone to get a need met. This presentation was probably more common in people who lived in the old institutional hospitals than it is now in the community. People may have been placed there as very young children and there were very low staffing rates meaning that people were not able to make attachments and therefore have an attachment figure to partner them in the process of emotional development.

Someone stuck at the practising stage of emotional development may practise the behaviours that are available to them over and over again; that is, rocking or shouting out words or screaming. They may be described as having "stereotypical behaviours". At this stage, any interactions are still very self-referenced in terms of having a need they want meeting, rather than being interested in two-way interactions. In adults with disabilities, we see practising behaviour often in people with profound disabilities, who engage in repetitive behaviours, in the absence of any progress to further skill development. One of the features of practising behaviours is that they do not appear to be goal directed, but exist in their own right, as a behaviour that is engaged in purely and simply because it is possible to do it. These behaviours are commonly seen in autistic people.

Someone who is stuck at the early rapprochement stage may be labelled as "attention seeking" as they are more active in seeking and wanting interaction and attention from others. There is a distinct reduction in the passivity seen in the early stages. They are at the emotional stage where they are seeking to practise their two-way interactional skills as well as negotiation skills. They may be labelled as being demanding of staff in their quest to get this need met and may engage in a range of behaviours which are perceived negatively, again in an attempt to get this need met.

At the late rapprochement stage, the person is testing out boundaries and their place in the world. People can seem to be very demanding and difficult to support at this stage. They may be more determined to get their need for interaction met as well as striving to establish their sense of self with those around them.

The TIC model has used Mahler's description of behaviours present at each emotional development stage to be able to understand the stage of development that an individual has achieved. Their development may have become arrested at this stage. Identifying that a thirty-year-old person with a learning disability is functioning at an emotional developmental stage of a two-year-old, and is in the early rapprochement stage, can greatly assist in the development of an appropriate therapeutic intervention for that person.

How to determine the stage of development someone is at

Frankish has developed an interval observation methodology to determine the stage of emotional development that an individual is at. Once trained in the method an observer completes the observation assessment over a forty-minute period. Frankish initially thought that the observations needed to be repeated across a number of different settings, but has found that this does not increase the reliability or validity of observations. Therefore, the observation process can be completed in one forty minute session. Analysis is then undertaken to establish the frequency of behaviours in each of the different stages. This analysis will then indicate the stage of emotional development that the person is at.

The same behaviour at different stages of emotional development

It has also been possible to identify that a specific type of behaviour can belong to all four of the developmental stages depending on its meaning. To give an example, the behaviour of head-banging can occur at each development stage. It looks the same at each stage, but has a different meaning. The child or adult who is functioning at the differentiation phrase will be head-banging in a self-stimulatory away, because they can. The person who is head-banging at the practising stage will be doing so because it is behaviour that they have discovered they can do and another behaviour hasn't yet appeared to take its place. The person who is head-banging at the early rapprochement phase is trying to communicate something to another person and has some belief in the fact that the other person is paying attention. The person who is head-banging at the late rapprochement phase is expressing a view that somebody better come and sort things out immediately.

It is only by carrying out a detailed observation that it is possible to identify the meaning of a particular person's behaviour. It is however crucial that this is done, as the response to the behaviour will vary according to the stage of development the person is at. More detail appears in the next chapter.

Interventions

In all cases where is has been identified that a person has not achieved individuation, the availability of a reliable and consistent significant other is crucial for helping the person to develop emotionally and in ending any problematic behaviours that are being expressed.

This may mean the development of a "core group" of carers who will be drawn upon to ensure that the person is always supported by someone from the core group. This enables the person to develop a trust in and attachment to their carers so providing the partner that is needed in the emotional development process. The intensity of the interaction between the person and their carer will vary depending at which stage they are at, but the crucial part is that the person knows, or is helped to understand over time, that there is someone reliably there for them who they have a positive and trusting relationship with. The carer does not need to be with the person the whole time, but does need to let the person know if they are going somewhere else and are not going to be immediately available and when they will return. This will all contribute to providing the emotional security for the person that is the basis of their potential to develop.

At the differentiation stage, the person is as emotionally vulnerable as a young child and can be easily overwhelmed. Therefore interaction with the significant other needs to be low demand, but consistent. An example might be a core staff member who lets the person know, at the beginning of the shift that they are there for them, and who periodically brings them a cup of tea or something else they like but does not demand any interaction from the person. The core staff member needs to be available to meet the person's needs when they arise. In terms of helping the person progress in their emotional development, the carer may gently introduce activities done together, that encourage the person to explore the world outside themselves, such as when going for a walk, pointing things out, or looking at books or activities together. The activities should be low demand on the individual and more about encouraging interest in the wider world but doing this together.

At the practising stage, the core staff member should still be non-demanding and be there to meet the person's needs, but may be able to encourage widening the repertoire of behaviours that the person has, gradually introducing them to and teaching them other activities. Also important is attending and paying attention to the things the person is doing, perhaps showing this overtly by commenting in a non-demanding way on what is happening.

In the early rapprochement stage, the person will be more demanding of staff, seeking attention in a more active way. This stage is about developing two-way relationship skills and therefore the core staff could get the person involved in activities that are two-way, that is, turn-taking activities. The carer can also encourage the person to do things together, for example laying the table together, folding the washing together, in fact any activity where there is interaction and a chance to practise and develop two-way communication and relationship skills.

At the late rapprochement stage, the person is going to be more demanding and challenging to support. The presence of a significant other who the person is attached to is still vitally important until they have become psychologically separate. However, the person may not need this carer all the time, but rather just need to know where the carer is. They may be demanding and challenging of the carers, who themselves may need support to allow tolerance of this stage. The person will be pushing for increased independence and needs to be guided towards this in an emotionally secure setting which monitors safety both physical and psychological.

To return to the person who is banging their head. If it is identified that they are at the differentiation phase they need to be given lots of non-demanding, gentle attention by a carer they have an attachment to and also the opportunity to explore their current or even different environment. The person who is banging their head at the practising stage needs to be encouraged to learn a new skill, within the context of a safe attachment relationship and increase the things they can do beyond banging their head. The person who is head-banging at the early rapprochement phase is probably expressing some anxiety or needs which should be addressed. It is crucial that at this stage the person has certainty about who is there for them on a daily basis to enable them to develop security that they are being supported by people who can assist them in terms of their needs but also their skill development. The person who is head-banging at the late rapprochement phase needs to be helped to find better ways of communicating their needs.

This approach is fundamentally different from some behavioural methods. Historically, a behavioural approach may have advocated ignoring the inappropriate behaviour and reinforcing only appropriate behaviour. In severely emotionally disabled people, this type of behavioural approach would be experienced as persecutory. Certainly the person who is arrested at the differentiation stage or practising stage of development does not have a sense of existing unless they are seen by another person. Ignoring the person's behaviour would certainly not give them this sense of being seen. More recent, positive behavioural approaches would look for the meaning of the behaviour. The Frankish Model adds an extra dimension to this consideration in terms of an understanding of the emotional development of the individual being the context from within to understand their behaviour.

Conclusion

This chapter has examined the work of Margaret Mahler and the influence of her findings on the development of the Frankish model. The work has once again shown the profound importance of the early years of life in a person's emotional development. This development is very much a two-way process and fraught with potential difficulty. Fortunately, most people progress through these stages without major mishap. However, the child who is ill, disabled, or in some other way distressed during this stage, will influence the ability of the parent to meet his needs. We have seen that it is possible through the use of trained observations to identify the stage of emotional development that an individual has been able to reach. It is also possible through observation to recognise when there is a relaxed non-anxious interaction between child and parent, or in adult situations between adult and caregiver. Similarly, observations reveal when there is only a superficiality between the two parties, and the consequent anxiety and/or distress that follows from this. Frankish's clinical experience has found that a large number of people who are described as having challenging behaviour, actually have a major schism in their interactions with others and a lack of any type of attachment relationship in their life to assist them in their emotional development.

One of the most exciting aspects of the Frankish model has been the realisation that it is possible to facilitate growth through the stages, and to measure the development of this over time. The model offers the opportunity to obtain scientific data around what is basically a psychodynamic approach. Although this work has been undertaken with adults and children with learning disabilities, it clearly is relevant to all development.

CHAPTER FOUR

Measuring the emotional development of intellectually disabled adults

Following on from the previous chapters we come to the need to apply the knowledge to help people who have suffered trauma in early childhood, and often again in later life. We find that double trauma (or more) is very common in the people with complex behaviour. The process for establishing a method for gathering the appropriate information to define an intervention is described below.

Adults with intellectual disability and severe behavioural disturbance have been shown to have emotional developmental delay. This can be measured and the stage of arrested development identified. Once identified, an intervention can be designed to address the problem and promote further development. Research has shown that it is possible to train non-professional staff to make the measurement with good inter-rater reliability. A consensus of professionals has established the validity of the measure. More than 100 people have benefited from the approach, which is based on the practical application of psychoanalytic stage theory described by Mahler.

After a long period of expecting behavioural approaches to solve all behavioural problems, there is now a growing recognition that feelings and emotional trauma may underpin behavioural disturbance (Royal College of Psychiatrists, 2004; Jahoda et al., 2001). There is, therefore, a need for an assessment of emotional development that can define and inform therapeutic interventions as well as measure change over time.

Behavioural assessments tend to be based on frequency and severity of behaviours labelled as maladaptive for the individual, or the setting in which they live. The purpose of the assessment is to identify the behaviour, the antecedents and consequences, then design an intervention to eradicate or modify the behaviour. These behaviours can be very severe in nature, often involving harm to self or others. Behaviours that are frequent and not too severe, for example persistent touching, respond quite well to this sort of intervention. However, behaviours that are low frequency but high intensity are less amenable because there are fewer opportunities to intervene and the consequences of the behaviour could be severe. Individuals with the second pattern may find themselves escalating to secure provision because of the severity of what they do, but usually without an appropriate intervention because of the difficulties of implementing a reinforcement or reward schedule. Some cognitive treatments are becoming more widely used with people with mild intellectual disability with some success (Lindsay et al., 1996; Taylor et al., 2002; Kroese et al., 1997). There is still a complex group for whom cognitive or behavioural approaches have limited usefulness. They frequently find themselves stuck in the secure system, usually because their behaviour is not understood. The emotional component would appear to be the missing link in understanding the meaning of the behaviours and possible intervention.

High-frequency, low-intensity behaviours, that is, those that cause irritation rather than fear, lend themselves better to behavioural interventions in segregated environments (Sturmey, 2008). The ability to engage in such an intervention depends on the skill of the staff group and the motivation of the service user. It is notable that people who remain in residential services for long periods usually exhibit these types of behaviours. They are still prevented, by their behaviour, from enjoying an ordinary life in an ordinary street. The intervention is of limited value in addressing the behaviour without looking at the meaning. There are many professionals and carers who still view the ability of intellectually disabled people to work with meaning to be unrealistic. There is, however, a growing body of knowledge to support the need to acknowledge and work with the inner emotional world.

If the behaviour can be seen from the point of view of the level of emotional development it may be possible to plan an intervention that enables the behaviour to change, and the person to grow in maturity. Frankish (1989, 1992) described such an approach, building on the work of Valerie Sinason (2010). The Frankish model now includes tools for measuring the emotional developmental stage and for planning interventions. The model is based on the emotional developmental stages described by Mahler et al. (1979, see previous chapter) in her work with young children. These stages were noticed in adults with intellectual disability and led to the development of the model. The model is described below. It is augmented by Winnicott's (1965) ideas of good enough parenting and consequent effective personality development.

The Frankish model, revisiting what is to be measured

Margaret Mahler, with her colleagues Pine and Bergman (1979), studied children with their primary carers for the first five years of their lives. They identified changes in behaviour that could be linked with stages of emotional development, and of changing from one stage to the next. They described the process as the process of moving from biological birth to psychological birth, and established that this happens in healthy development at about the age of thirty-six to forty months. With psychological birth comes the sense of self as separate from others, with manageable anxiety. The stages are described in more detail in the previous chapter but summarised here for clarity:

Symbiotic, where there is no noticeable difference between mother and child, as if they are still joined. This is only seen in the first few weeks of life.

Differentiation, where the child is beginning to notice parts of himself and the immediate surroundings. This is a self-referenced stage and lasts until about the age of eight to ten months in ordinary development. The child is dependent on the carer for external input, and responds to this as opposed to initiating it.

Practising, which occurs as the child becomes able to do more things. Each new skill is practised until competence is reached and then becomes part of the repertoire, with a new one taking its place.

Practising behaviours continue to dominate up to the age of about fifteen months and the range increases with parental attention, and decreases without this attention.

Early rapprochement, where the child begins to initiate some two-way interaction, usually corresponding with the beginnings of motor and vocal skills. Parental structure is necessary for this to be navigated successfully. It lasts from about fifteen to twenty-four months. During this stage and the next, a "looking" behaviour is frequently used to facilitate "emotional refuelling".

Late rapprochement, where the child begins to be able to be separate from the parent or carer for a greater distance and a longer time, with manageable anxiety. Parent or carer support is needed to facilitate this development of independence at the appropriate rate to ensure that anxiety remains manageable, and independence increases. This stage lasts from about twenty-four to thirty-six months and leads to a "rapprochement crisis" and individuation. This is the point at which the sense of self as a separate person is established. Once this individuation is reached it is not lost. Although later trauma may lead to emotional difficulties, they will be qualitatively different from those that are seen in people who have been traumatised pre-individuation.

Comparable behaviours are frequently seen in adults with intellectual disabilities who display behavioural difficulties. For example, someone who bangs their head while taking no notice of anyone watching will be exercising practising behaviour. They do it because they can and another, more suitable, behaviour has not become available to them. If they bang and look to see if someone is watching, it is an early rapprochement behaviour and meant to communicate something. If banging and looking at the observer with the clear intent of making the observer do something, then it is late rapprochement. The stages encapsulate the process of emotional development that leads towards clear two-way interaction, and the later stages moving towards exerting control of the situation. If the meaning of the behaviour can be established in this way, and the developmental stage, it is possible to begin to plan an effective intervention. Using behavioural approaches, like differential reinforcement of other behaviours (DRO) cannot be effective unless the person is sufficiently emotionally mature to care about the consequences, or the approval of the observer. Consequently, DRO will not work with people at the differentiation or practising level, and is not really effective until late rapprochement or individuation.

The difficulty with the earlier stages is that any ignoring of behaviour will be experienced as abandonment or persecution and create more distress.

The measurement technique

In order to take the theory forward, it was necessary to find an efficient way to arrive at the developmental stage. Clearly, anything cumbersome or dependent on clinical judgement would have limited usefulness. Initially a continuous observation was employed to work out the developmental stage, and this resulted in a large quantity of data to analyse but would reach a conclusion. The second approach was to observe for twenty seconds and write for forty seconds, always observing the same twenty seconds in each minute. This provided the same answer and was less intensive. The third question was about how long the observation needed to be to secure the right answer. Participants were observed in several different locations, where the opportunities for behaviours were wide and varied, and the same developmental stage was found, even if the types of behaviour were different. Experiments were then done to determine the length of observation required and this was established to be forty minutes (Frankish, 1992).

Extensive further work, using naive observers, was undertaken to establish the efficacy of the method for wider use. This involved participants in the community and, also, in a restricted environment. The observers were psychology graduates with no specific other experience with the client group or method. They were instructed in the process for gathering the data. The inter-rater reliability was assessed with the Kappa statistic, the most commonly used coefficient in the medical literature for this purpose (Viera & Garratt, 2005). There were two aspects to inter-rate, the actual observations, and the agreed stage of development from the observations, the latter being the most important for the purpose. The Kappa scores were moderate to perfect on the observed behaviours and 100 per cent on the identified stage. This provides robust support for the use of the measurement method with a naive observer.

The next issue was validity. In the absence of another measure to use, it was evident that a consensus of professionals was the only acceptable method for establishing validity. A group was assembled and met three times. On each occasion, they were presented with case material and asked to bring their own. A wide range of cases were examined and discussed. It was unanimously agreed that the measure was measuring what it purported to measure (Frankish, 2013a).

Once observers have become competent in their observing skill, they can use the measure on a form that allocates the stage at the same time as making the observation. However, as this does not leave a second opportunity for examination with supervision, it is only used by very experienced people.

The stage of development is allocated to the highest number of scores in that category from the forty data points. There will always be some scatter but there is always a dominant score. Occasionally there will be two scores that are not too far apart and these have been shown through practice to indicate someone in the process of moving from one stage to the next. Where this occurs, the intervention is directed at the lower level with the expectation that progress will be quite rapid.

Use in practice

The measurement technique has been used in a wide variety of settings, from community to high-security (Frankish, 2000). I have specialised in assessing individuals with complex behaviours. The assessment always includes other measures of ability, mental health, and self-esteem. The observation is added and can usually supply the missing data that will explain the complex behaviours of the individual. There are strong links between some of the types of referral and the identified developmental stages. For example, an individual with a mild intellectual disability and described as manipulative will usually be identified as early rapprochement in terms of their emotional self. The manipulation is a cry for recognition and support, not control. Once this is recognised and a more nurturing regime put in place, further development occurs and the individual improves significantly. There are similar findings with obsessive behaviours. They are typically practising behaviours and indicate the need for a high level of support as this equates to the age-equivalent of approximately one year old. Again, an intervention that is constant, reliable, and supportive will produce excellent results, and very quickly.

It is important to ensure that the observation is carried out thoroughly as it is possible to misinterpret behaviours from a short observation. Some of them look similar until examined more closely. The most common error is to consider a withdrawn person to have reached individuation and to be self-contained. It is only through careful observation of what happens when they do interact, that the right stage can be identified, which is probably practising, and the person has "shut down" through lack of attention. All of these stages relate to developmental stages that are pre-individuation. This means an emotional age of less than three years. Any child or adult who is less than three emotionally, needs to receive consistent and nurturing care and support. If the stage is wrongly identified, the intervention can become persecutory and the behaviour will deteriorate. This frequently leads to escalation to secure settings. It is not uncommon to find detained people engaging in behaviour that results in restraint in order to receive some human contact.

Once the stage has been identified, it is possible to design an intervention that provides the necessary emotional environment in which progress can be made (Frankish, 1992). This involves naming a "significant other" at all times, so that the individual being supported always knows who it is. This results in an immediate reduction in anxiety. Clearly, it is not possible to have the same person for 24 hours a day so a team must be established, with a formal changeover at shift change in the presence of the person being supported. Visual cards can be used to identify who is coming next. The member of staff does not have to work in a close one-to-one situation all the time, but must be available, and tell "their" person where they are going if they have to leave for a short time.

After establishing the staff group and the organised regime, the next part involves enabling the individual to move on to the next stage. The way this is done depends on the starting point. If they are at the differentiation stage, they will do very little to initiate interaction or activities. The member of staff then needs to approach at regular intervals and initiate something, but without asking anything of them. After a few days, the individual will start looking for the approach. From this they can be encouraged to try an activity and practising behaviours can become established. If at the practising stage, they can be introduced to two-way interaction and so on. Once people have reached late rapprochement they can begin to reason and plan, and will be more demanding. It is only when they reach full individuation that they have a full sense of their own agency and can function more independently.

Results of interventions

Interventions are successful and often quite rapid. Once the anxiety is relieved, development occurs, leading to curiosity and more learning. Interaction is particularly improved and emotional growth becomes obvious to all. It then becomes possible to offer more opportunities for wider experiences and the quality of life improves. It has been noted that the movement from one stage to another takes approximately the same time as it would in natural development, implying that early intervention would prevent some of the distressed behaviours that are seen.

The success of the model leads to questions about the reason for the arrested emotional development. As the problem can be addressed reasonably easily, the question must be posed as to why it has not been addressed before. Studying historical notes, or interviewing families, reveals the information that the arrested emotional development is linked to traumatic events in early childhood. All individuals with whom this approach has been used have experienced an event in early childhood that has left them stuck at the relevant stage of emotional development. It seems that no further personality development occurs after the traumatic event unless there is an appropriate intervention. Physical and cognitive development is less affected by the trauma, but there have been instances of improvement in cognitive function, once the emotional needs are met.

Conclusions

The study has shown that it is possible to measure the emotional developmental stage that an individual has reached, and this can be used to design an intervention to facilitate development and change, leading to improved quality of life. The model is based on stage theory of emotional development with a practical application. The development of the self with agency is essential for individuals with intellectual disabilities if they want to have as independent a life as they are capable of.

Discussion

This work has been in progress for over twenty years and only some of it has been previously submitted for publication, although more has been presented orally at conferences. The individuals for whom the approach has been most useful have sometimes been easily identifiable, making it inappropriate to make public the findings. It is hoped that this book will make the model more widely known and available for use.

The coded measure is available from Frankish Training, with training in its use.

CHAPTER FIVE

Other influences

There are some other key authors who have influenced the development of the model for trauma informed care. Each will be considered for their specific contribution to the thinking. They have lots more to offer in their own right and only a small portion of their impact on services generally will be covered here.

The first to consider is Freud. Without him, we would perhaps have waited many years to become aware of the unconscious and how unconscious processes influence what we do. It is the impact of trauma on the unconscious that leads to people becoming complex and in need of a specific way to understand them. No amount of applied behaviour analysis will lead to accessing the inner world of a distressed person. Accepting that all behaviour has meaning and the skill is in finding that meaning takes us to the ideas that Freud put forward. He didn't link specifically with people with disabilities, or even with children, but making the point about everyone having an inner world is immensely valuable. He also broke down the psyche into the id, ego and superego and these terms continue to be useful at times. We may not use the terms but we will be aware of levels of maturity that indicate ego development and of people who are persecuted by their conscience (superego).

The next person to think about is Melanie Klein. She was not scientific and her work is rejected by many, as a consequence. However, she gave us some ideas that have been really useful. One is that all babies are born angry, with murderous rage. This helps us to understand the primary anger that we see sometimes where there has been no attachment figure to aid socialisation. This idea fits very well with Winnicott's work on primary development. These are the main two theorists who have addressed primary development and they have contributed greatly to the understanding of the more complex people who appear to be functioning as babies in adult bodies. Klein also gave us the breakdown of the developmental processes of the developing mind, from the paranoid schizoid position of early childhood, to the depressive position of those who have come to a stage of being able to manage their anxiety. This makes so much sense of those individuals who cannot tolerate change, decision making, or uncertainty. Once we accept that they have not had an adequate early experience to become able to "know", it is easier and more acceptable to work with where they are.

Later on, Fairbairn (1954) developed the ideas of object relations. There is a later chapter on assessment using the object relations technique. The theory is introduced here. It builds on Klein's work, who was the first to refer to objects when thinking about the development of early relationships. So, the first object that the child relates to is the mother or primary carer, the one who feeds. Klein speaks about part-objects and refers to the breast as the first relationship. In object relations terms, the baby introjects the first object and then has a mental view of himself from his own perspective and another view of himself from the perspective of the first relationship. This then becomes the two-person level. After that a second person/object is introjected and then the three-person level is reached. Clearly, this is not a process that can be quantified but can be seen in a baby observation. The child is then building up a picture of himself internally that relates to how others see it. This process continues throughout life and there is truth in the statement that we are a product of every one-to-one relationship we have ever had. With each new object of our affections or attention, we take in some of how others see us. So the child who has always received love and care will grow up feeling lovable and worthy of others' affections. The child who has grown up with neglect and hatred will grow up feeling unloved and unwanted.

Carl Rogers (1951) gave us the term person-centred therapy. It is difficult for us now to think of any other sort as the approach has filtered through to all other models of therapy to some extent. There are still some therapies that rely on the therapist as expert giving directions for the client to follow. There are some totally non-directive therapies that may leave the client quite lost and seeking direction. The idea of being person centred is that the therapist adjusts the approach to match the person they are working with, so not too directive and not too non-directive. From the point of view of complex traumatised people, this means being aware of how scared they are, holding them emotionally and listening to their own story, in whatever form that story is told. Some people will only be able to tell the story through actions and their behaviour will demonstrate how they are feeling. Others will use words but they may be heavily defended against reality, giving an unclear picture of what really happened, or so hurt that any attempt to speak about it involves them dissolving into incapability. Being person centred means being patient, listening carefully, giving unconditional regard, and making sure that both minds are working for the benefit of the client.

The people considered so far have all worked with adults and children of average intelligence or above. None of them specialised in working with people with intellectual disabilities. Our next author to consider is Valerie Sinason, who now works with people with dissociative identity disorder (DID), but has been for many years a leader in the field of disability psychotherapy. Her book *Mental Handicap and the Human Condition* (2010) has been reprinted and is widely read across the world. Valerie began working psychodynamically with children with disabilities in an educational setting and decided to train as a child analyst. In her role as a child analyst at the Tavistock, she was asked to see adults with learning disabilities, the assumption being that they were functioning as children. She knew this to be not so, having had a broad experience of disability in her childhood. Her father was a leader in the field of provision for people with disabilities. Having established a caseload of people she began to support the Mental Handicap Workshop, as it was called. This was a group set up at the Tavistock by Neville Symington in the early 1980s to support professionals working in the field of mental handicap as it was then called. Interestingly, one of the points that Valerie speaks about is the frequent change of name. Just during the 1900s, the name changed from moron to imbecile to mental deficiency to mental sub-normality to learning disability. And now, in the 2000s, we use the term intellectual disability. The term learning difficulty had usually been reserved for educational issues.

Valerie continued to work at the Tavistock seeing adults and children with disabilities, and then went to work at St. George's, University of London, with Professor Sheila Hollins. Together they pioneered group work in the community with quite complex people. This psychotherapy group is a slow, open group, and continues to this day, with a range of therapists, all committed to providing a growth experience in a safe therapeutic setting.

Secondary handicap is a term that Valerie has made available to us. This refers to the mechanism whereby people will be more or differently disabled, in order to hide the learning disability. So, people would rather be labelled alcoholic than learning disabled. Some will accentuate their disability and this is experienced aggressively by others. I remember a young boy with hemiplegia who would always sit so that others had to look at his damaged side. He struggled with his good side and bad side and had to make sure that his bad side could be tolerated by others. But it was presented angrily as if to say, "Look at me, I'm disabled." Others will make their speech less intelligible than it needs to be to make the listener work harder.

The handicapped smile is another feature that Valerie has observed and written about. This refers to the habit of smiling even while hurting. Disabled people do it to ward off attack and to apologise for being there. It is particularly noticeable in people with Down Syndrome, who gain a reputation for always being happy, when, in fact, sometimes they are very unhappy but know that they are more acceptable if they smile. The smiling is a defence for the individual and a protection from pain for the observer.

Sheila Hollins and Valerie Sinason published a short paper in 2000 where they listed the core issues that are there for every disabled person who engages in uncovering psychotherapy. These are sex, death, abandonment, and the pain of difference.

Issues about sex, being made by bad sex, being unacceptable as a sexual partner, gender confusion, and such like, occur frequently in the psyche of people with intellectual disabilities. This is often linked with the knowledge that they could have, or should have, been aborted, which further links with loss and death. During personal relationship group therapy, it is often the case that someone will raise the issue that they could have been an abortion with mixed feelings about how they are valued in their family.

Death is a common theme in all psychotherapy. It is not uncommon for it to be assumed that people with disabilities have no or different emotions and will not be affected by death. This is, of course, not the case, and the loss of a parent or close relative will have a massive impact. Many people are also aware that their families may wish they hadn't been born and they experience "death-making" (Wolfensberger, 1972); that sense of being treated as less than human, with fewer rights of existence. Everyone has an experience of loss when, as a small child, they suddenly realise they are on their own (individuation), but people with disabilities may have been sent to school very early, before they are able to keep their parent in mind, and have had multiple placements, each move resulting in the loss of people they know and care about.

Feelings of abandonment can link all the way back to being left in hospital at birth, nowadays in a special care baby unit, but in the past, may have been left to the care of the state. We can't be sure about how much is processed in the immature brain but we do know, from clinical work with people at later stages that they are often left with a vague feeling of not belonging. The incidence of divorce in families with a disabled child is higher than the average, indicating more disruption and being left. In therapeutic encounters, this fear is played out by attempts to prolong the session and not let the therapist leave. Also with distress at shift changeover times, and when staff leave, or a placement move happens.

The biggest issue is about the pain of difference. This is always a focus of therapy at some stage. Often defended against, individuals will stress how "normal" they are, how they can do and be all sorts of things, refusing to accept that they can't. An example would be the young man who goes to the day service centre in a suit and carrying a briefcase, as if going to work in the city. Another would be a young woman wearing the height of fashion even though the clothes don't fit and don't suit her. The urge to fit in and be like others is very strong. Therapy would aim to help them to be happy being who they are, not seeking to be someone else. Being able to be with someone, as they face the feelings of acceptance of the real self, and giving up the false self, is very moving and respectful of their individuality.

Valerie continues to speak and publish work, and to help out in South Africa with services for traumatised disabled people there. She has spent her career campaigning for better services for disabled people.

Brett Kahr (2008) is another author who has added to the knowledge base. He has worked primarily with sexual issues and has added to our understanding of how the emotional difficulties associated with disability can lead to an inappropriate or troublesome display of sexuality. It is not uncommon for learning-disabled offenders to be permanently supervised and some will need this. Brett has put forward ways of recognising when the offending is a distortion of an attachment issue and can be addressed in therapy.

There is a wide range of information from other perspectives, such as applied behaviour analysis, positive behaviour support, cognitive behaviour therapy, and social learning theory. These all have their place in disability services but have significantly less relevance for the complex people who need trauma-informed care. They are mentioned here to show that they are not discounted, but considered and found to not add to the understanding required to work at the deeper level of the self.

CHAPTER SIX

Designing interventions

Introduction

After we have taken into account the emotional needs of an individual, we need to plan to provide support that will both meet the needs and facilitate more development. We will have identified the emotional developmental stage and usually have an idea of what traumatic events need to be processed. Each intervention will be very individual but there are some general guidelines that help with the planning and execution.

Interventions

People who have suffered early trauma in their lives are frequently functioning at the pre-individuation level. People with intellectual disabilities will be more at risk of early separations and interference in the two-way interaction processes that are essential for healthy emotional development.

In all cases where is has been identified that a person has not achieved individuation, the availability of a reliable and consistent significant other is crucial for helping the person to develop emotionally and in assisting with any problematic behaviours that are being expressed.

A substitute significant other

Providing a substitute significant other is essential for providing an emotionally supportive environment. This may mean that we have to develop a "core group" of carers who will be drawn upon to ensure that the person is always supported by someone from the core group. This enables the person to develop a trust in, and attachment to, their carers, so providing the partner that is needed in the emotional development process. The intensity of the interaction between the person and their carer will vary depending at which stage they are at, but the crucial part is that the person knows, or is helped to understand over time, that there is someone reliably there for them with whom they have a positive and trusting relationship. The carer does not need to be with the person the whole time, but does need to let the person know if they are going somewhere else and are not going to be immediately available and when they will return. This will all contribute to providing the emotional security for the person that is the basis of their potential to develop.

The early stage—differentiation

At the differentiation stage, the person is as emotionally vulnerable as a young child and can be easily overwhelmed. Therefore interaction with the significant other needs to be low demand, but consistent. An example might be a core staff member who lets the person know, at the beginning of the shift that they are there for them, and who periodically brings them a cup of tea or something else they like but does not demand any interaction from the person. The core staff member needs to be available to meet the person's needs when they arise. In terms of helping the individual progress in their emotional development, the carer may gently introduce activities done together, that encourage the person to explore the world outside themselves, such as when going for a walk pointing things out or looking at books or activities together. The activities should be low demand on the individual and more about encouraging interest in the wider world but doing this together.

Someone who is more cognitively able and may have completed the house-tree-person test (HTP) or the object relations technique (ORT), indicating the one-person stage of development, will still need the same level of emotional support, but may be able to engage in more talking and activities. They are likely to be quite cut-off and not expecting to have a relationship. A number of autistic people will fall into this group, thinking especially of those who do not see the point of other people. The aim of the contact, and the reliability, is to help them to look outside of themselves and see another person, then to move on to see that the other person may be able to improve their life. Once they start to look for the other person, their named significant other, they are beginning to engage and will be able to move on to the next stage.

The second stage—practising

At the practising stage, the core staff member is still very much present and not asking anything of the individual they are supporting. The key feature of always being available is continued. The staff member should still be non-demanding and be there to meet the individual's needs. Once the basic needs are met, there may now be energy for the beginnings of exploration of the world. This leads to the widening of the repertoire of behaviours that the person has. So, for example, when carrying out a task, the staff member will say what they are doing out loud, so that there is the potential for exposure to things not noticed in the past, the development of interest, and then action. Also important is attending and paying attention to the things the person is initiating themselves, perhaps showing this overtly by commenting in a non-demanding way on what is happening. It will be noticed that any new activity undertaken will be repeated and repeated. This is practising. It will continue until another behaviour becomes available. It is quite common to see people who are stuck at the practising stage, engaging in the same activity all day. They become known as "the one who rocks" or "the one who rattles the window catch". They are individuals who have made some progress on the road to individuation but have lacked the emotional support necessary for further development, so have become stuck. It may be that they were separated from their primary carer before they were ready, taken to the child development centre, or nursery, and became so anxious that they shut down emotionally. It will have been observed but, generally, attributed to the intellectual disability, which is understandable, but has the effect of limiting the development.

Moving on to rapprochement

Rapprochement is a big word for give and take. It is all about two-way interaction. Inevitably, this needs the availability of another person. The significant other is essential to the continuation of the developmental process. It is often a delight to realise that an individual with intellectual disability is making a stand for what they want. But it can, of course, also be daunting. The joy of learning during the practising stage moves on to a more challenging stage as the individuality begins to be established.

In the early rapprochement stage the person will be more demanding of staff, seeking attention in a more active way. This stage is about developing two-way relationship skills and therefore the core staff could get the person involved in activities that are two-way, that is, turn-taking activities. The significant other can also encourage the person to do things together, for example laying the table together, folding the washing together and other domestic chores. Any activity where there is interaction and a chance to practise and develop two-way communication and relationship skills is valuable. Games like Connect-4, ball games and such like are ideal. There will be an increase in eye contact, more face reading, more interest in the other person as development progresses. There will be more issues at shift change time, as the sense of loss is experienced. This needs to be handled sensitively with recognition that previous abandonment feelings are being activated. The handover from one person to the next must be done in the presence of the individual being supported, so they can see both people at once, and make the transfer of attachment and feelings of safety in a shared encounter. Some people will still struggle and try to make their chosen person stay with them, but it is part of their development that they manage to tolerate the loss of one and the arrival of the other.

Nearly there

The rapprochement stage takes quite a long time to navigate completely, probably two years or more. There is a gradual move along a continuum from noticing the presence of another person as useful, through to reaching a point of not needing the other person.

At the late rapprochement stage, the person is going to be more demanding and challenging to support. The presence of a significant other, the attachment figure, is still vitally important until they have become psychologically separate. However, the person may not need this carer all the time, but rather just need to know where the carer is. They may be demanding and challenging of the carers, who themselves may need support to allow tolerance of this stage. The individual will be pushing for increased independence and needs to be guided towards this in an emotionally secure setting which monitors safety, both physical and psychological.

There is lots of negotiation at this stage. The use of "if then" becomes possible, negotiating that "if you do this, then the other can happen". When the individual being supported starts to say it, there is evidence of real progress. Delayed gratification becomes possible, working for a treat that comes later. The ability to think and to reason develops rapidly in this stage, together with a growing awareness of the rights and needs of others. It is only at the late rapprochement stage that we can expect any consideration of others. Prior to this, the individual is very egocentric and unable to think that others have needs. This can often be a problem at the early stages, when others feel that they are being "let off" from responsibility.

There is then a rapprochement crisis, when the point of individuation is reached. Of course, not everyone manages to individuate. People who reach late rapprochement do have a better quality of life than those who don't. Individuals who have an intellectual disability may never be able to be completely separate because of their need for support for other reasons. However, they may be able to move on to less support, once they have the emotional capacity to ask, wait, and tolerate things going wrong. Those that do reach the rapprochement crisis will do so either with a big tantrum, or a quiet acceptance that they are on their own. It is the point at which they realise and accept that they can manage their anxiety when there is no one to ask.

The same behaviour at different stages

Let us consider the person who is banging his head. If it is identified that he is at the differentiation stage, he needs to be given lots of non-demanding, gentle attention by the significant other, and also the opportunity to explore his current or even different environments. The head banging will be happening as a self-stimulatory and explorative behaviour, not related to the presence of anyone. If it is gentle and not harmful, it can be commented on with a simple awareness-raising statement like "I can see that you can bang your head". This can be followed up with "I wonder what else you can do". The purpose is not to get him to do anything else, but to raise awareness of the possibility. At this stage, he is unable to care about the effect on others.

The person who is banging his head at the practising stage needs to be encouraged to learn a new skill, within the context of a safe attachment relationship and increase the things he can do beyond banging his head. So in this situation there would be building on the awareness from the previous stage and begin to teach new skills. At first, the activities will be made available, and then the individual encouraged to look at them, touch and try. Interest will increase, maybe even some eye contact, and things will be tried. Observations suggest that there is more activity if the significant other maintains the level of attention, and decreases if the attention wavers. Any skill that is carried out and distracts from the head banging is useful. There needs to be recognition that the head banging is being engaged in as a skill that the person has, and will only stop if it is replaced by another more interesting behaviour.

The person who is head banging at the early rapprochement phase is probably expressing some anxiety or needs that should be addressed. It is crucial that at this stage the person has certainty about who is there for him on a daily basis. This enables him to develop security that he is being supported by people who can assist him, in terms of his needs but also with his skill development. There is clear communication in the action, a clear message. Some people bang their heads because they are troubled by thoughts and anxieties. At this stage, there will be awareness of the role of the significant other and communication of the fear they feel if their person is not visible, or is busy with someone else. Many behaviours that are labelled challenging fall into this stage; seen as demanding and attention seeking. At this stage, the individual needs a lot of attention. He has reached a developmental stage of knowing that people are there for him, but has not reached the stage of being able to wait or consider the needs of others. If his needs are met, the challenging behaviour also stops. There is a strong sense of him not being able to trust that he will be safe if his significant other is not close.

The person who is head banging at the late rapprochement phase is clearly communicating distress or powerlessness. He needs to be helped to find better ways of communicating his needs, using verbal communication if possible, or be given a picture board or communicator. The level and type of support at this stage will depend on the intellectual impairment. If quite severely disabled, he will need to be given clear methods of communication. He may also benefit from some individual work to address his feelings about being powerless, or his awareness of and pain about his disability. It has only been relatively recently that there has been acceptance of the usefulness of talking therapies for people with limited intellectual ability but, fortunately, these are now available. People who have mild disabilities can always benefit from talking therapies and, if almost individuated, may benefit from group therapy to help them reach that point of acceptance of being alone but connected.

How is it different from other approaches?

Behavioural methods

This approach is fundamentally different from some models. It concentrates completely on the development of a sense of self within the relationship with the significant other. Historically, a behavioural approach may have advocated ignoring the inappropriate behaviour and to reinforce only appropriate behaviour. In severely emotionally disabled people, this type of behavioural approach would be experienced as persecutory. Certainly the person who is arrested at the differentiation stage or practising stage of development does not have a sense of existing unless he is seen by another person. Ignoring the person's behaviour would certainly not give him this sense of being seen. It may be that some behaviours, especially those seen as stereotypical, have persisted for this reason. The individual is cut off from emotional contact and therefore continues only to do what he had learned before he shut down emotionally as a consequence of the lack of a reliable significant other.

Other approaches, using token reinforcers or cognitive methods, require that the person sees the value of what is offered. This is not possible at the early emotional developmental stages and so there can be a mismatch between the plan offered and the ability of the individual to recognise, accept or respond to it. Many behaviour plans have failed for this reason. However, there is room for the consistency of approach that is fundamental to behaviour plans. There is also some merit in the positive support that can be offered, so long as the meaning of the behaviour is worked out through observation and interaction.

All behaviour has meaning and a comprehensive plan for an intervention must take account of all the aspects. Behavioural approaches can be used for teaching new skills, making sure that what is presented as a reward is truly valued by the person learning. Trying to use conditioning approaches to correct behaviour that is seen as maladaptive doesn't generally work. This is usually because it is impossible to identify the meaning of the behaviour sufficiently well. All aspects of the person must be considered, and this may include some guesswork or speculation.

Cognitive methods

Cognitive approaches require that individuals can express something of their thoughts and feelings. These can be seen to be the cause of a behaviour and, if restructured, can lead to a change in behaviour. It is sometimes useful to speculate on what someone might be thinking and test it out. If the individual can speak, he can be asked what he was thinking during an incident or expression of distress. He may not have the words to explain and it may take time to arrive at an answer, but showing interest will help straight away. If there is little or no speech, it will be necessary to speculate and for carers to behave as if they understand, then see if it helps and, if confirmed, proceed on that basis. So, for example, if a young man is kicking a wall and hurting his foot we could speculate that he wants to kick someone else, that he is hurt or angry and thinking "I hate you, you don't care". Telling him to stop is unlikely to help. Telling him to stop hurting himself probably won't have an impact, except maybe to make him do it more. Saying "you look angry with someone" is likely to make him look round and pay attention because he feels understood. It is the recognition of the connection between thoughts and feelings that helps.

Psychodynamic and emotional considerations

If we think about what someone does being a consequence of how they feel, we move into the area of the emotional world, which includes consideration of unconscious processes, as well as conscious ones. We have covered the emotional developmental process but we need now to think about what traumatic events may have interrupted the natural progression to maturity. People often cannot say why they feel as they do, cannot access the shock and trauma that they have experienced. This is particularly true of events that happened in early childhood, always hard when it is at the pre-lingual stage and even harder for people with intellectual disabilities who may lack language skills. We are frequently looking for others to report if there were traumatic events in early life and, where families can be consulted, it is useful. Many people with very challenging behaviour have no family contact and this may be significant, as abandonment and separation are frequent causes of distressed behaviour.

An intervention based on these criteria will include individual therapy for the distressed individual, as well as the support of the significant other throughout the day. Information may be gathered via HTP and ORT, as well as a detailed history if it is available. The therapy will be weekly where possible and the pain addressed. Many people with intellectual disabilities have issues about difference to face, as well as abandonment, sexuality, death, and loss. They may have struggled more than others to process events that they have had no words for. They will be able to use the therapeutic process more effectively if they have the primary need for emotional security addressed as well.

Systemic approaches

Sometimes problem behaviour has a big impact on a system and sometimes a sick or disturbed system can have an impact on behaviour. Systems are complex and human systems more so than many others. The more people in a system the more complex it becomes. So, a simple dyad of two people can be the easiest but even that can have communication breakdown. A family system is one we are familiar with and we all know periods in our own families when things have been fraught and the system has either broken down or been in danger of doing so. The rate of divorce and reconstituted families in the twenty-first century is indicative of the difficulty in keeping systems going. It is stressors that lead to breakdown and identifying these is essential when planning an intervention. Sometimes it is the extreme behaviour that is the major stressor. Other times it is shortage of staff, inefficient or negative management, not enough money, or something as simple as the heating breaking down. The important thing to remember is that over-reaction to system stress is more likely to lead to permanent breakdown than anything else. Taking time out to work out what is the stressor, what impact is it having, what can be done to reduce it, will all be beneficial.

So, for example, a small group home for three people has a staff group of six people, and a manager who also manages five other homes. The individuals are living there because they are adult and it was time to leave the parental home. They also have a reputation for being very demanding and the staff don't generally choose to work in this home. If there is an incident one evening where someone gets hurt, the immediate reaction is often to send the offender to somewhere else, perhaps for admission to an assessment and treatment unit. This is usually an over-reaction. Asking an external person to look at the system and work out the dynamics can lead to an understanding that the man who lashed out was afraid because he couldn't understand why no one wanted to take him out, became distressed, when told to calm down felt more unloved and unwanted, so broke down and lashed out. There was no intent to hurt. There was a discharge of anxiety and distress. The staff present report that they were afraid that the situation might get out of control and tried to tighten up control. This is like capping a volcano. It is better to let it bubble over than to make it explode. By exploring what was happening it is possible to see how things could be different next time, everyone can agree to talk first when things are fraught, and the system can become competent at processing its own distress.

Conclusion

This chapter has examined the work of Margaret Mahler and the influence of her findings on the development of the model of trauma informed care. The work has once again shown the profound importance of the early years of life in a person's emotional development. This development is very much a two-way process and fraught with potential difficulty. Fortunately, most people progress through these stages without major mishap. However the child who is ill, disabled, or in some other way distressed during this stage, will influence the ability of the parent to meet his needs. We have seen that it is possible through the use of trained observations to identify the stage of emotional development that an individual has been able to reach. It is also possible through observation to recognise when there is a relaxed non-anxious interaction between child and parent, or in adult situations between adult and caregiver. Similarly, observations reveal the consequent anxiety and/or distress that follow from this when there is only a superficiality between the two parties. My clinical experience has found that a large number of people who are described as having challenging behaviour, actually have a major schism in their interactions with others and a lack of any type of attachment relationship in their life to assist them in their emotional development.

One of the most exciting aspects of the model has been the realisation that it is possible to facilitate growth through the stages, and to measure the development of this over time. The model offers the opportunity to obtain scientific data around what is basically a psychodynamic approach. Although this work has been undertaken with adults and children with learning disabilities, it clearly is relevant to all development.

CHAPTER SEVEN

The house-tree-person test

I first came across the house-tree-person test (HTP) in the late eighties. It had been developed at the Tavistock for use as a therapeutic tool for work with children. I liked the simplicity of it and the fact that people with intellectual disabilities could draw the pictures when they might not be able to do things that were more complex. So, I started to use it. I quickly realised that the individual gives away a lot of themselves in the drawings and that they must be treated with real respect. Since then, I have used it only for assessment and always put the drawings in a safe place, carefully labelled, so that we can ask for some more at a later date and use them in measuring change over time.

The drawings are drawn quickly and not lingered over. They come straight from the unconscious. People draw the same pictures repeatedly if they haven't changed, indicating that a change in the drawings indicates a change in the self.

The test must be administered correctly or it will be invalid. People are not told they are going to do the HTP. If they are, they will invariably draw all three on the same page and then the test is useless. Instead, they are presented with one sheet of paper and asked if they will please draw a house. Very few people refuse although often they will say that they are no good at drawing. They need to be encouraged to carry on, with reassurance that we are not looking at who can do the best drawing; it is their drawing that is important.

The house drawing is then taken away and turned over. Another sheet offered with the request to draw a tree. They may turn the paper for this and that's all right. Once the tree is drawn, it is taken away and turned out of sight. A third sheet is offered and they are asked to draw a person. Most people will attempt all three drawings. Some will be barely recognisable as what they are, but all will be different from each other.

When all three have been drawn, they are put away and the individual told that they will be looked at later. Another sheet can be offered with the invitation to draw whatever they would like to draw. This last drawing can be taken away by them, and talked about in the session. It is likely to give some insight into what they find interesting so may be a good stimulus for the session anyway.

The drawings are then looked at for examination and interpretation. The house is considered to be a reflection of the degree to which they feel grounded and have a basic sense of security. Most people draw a house the same way they would have drawn it when they first started school, square with a door and four windows, a roof and a chimney. Usually it will be central to the page and cover about two-thirds of the available space. If it is different from this, there is meaning in that difference. Some people draw lots of extra windows, or no door, or a chimney sticking out at the side. Lots of windows indicate some level of intrusion and possible abuse, no door indicates being trapped inside or prevented from getting inside. Some chimneys look phallic and may have smoke pouring out of them. See figures 1 and 2 for some examples.

The tree is indicative of the life force or ego. Ideally, it has a strong trunk, with branches and leaves in proportion to the trunk, and roots or implied roots, filling a significant part of the paper. Many people with intellectual disabilities will draw a tree that is stunted, or has a week trunk, or a limited top. What is often the case is that there is potential for ego development shown by the trunk but that it has been arrested at some stage and the top looks very impoverished (see figure 3). Similarly, there may be no roots, or implied roots, indicating a cutting off from the past. Sometimes the tree will have extras, like birds or fruit; sometimes there will be a single branch sticking out at the side. Other times there will be a hole in the trunk, that may look like a vagina. It follows that issues of sexuality and sexual feelings or sexual identity will begin to show in the tree drawing. Also, we do see split-off parts, indicating parts of the ego that are separated off for whatever reason (see figure 4). This may be a representation of psychosis or dissociation. It will usually be the first indication of difficulties with the development of self, and this may be confirmed with the person drawing.

The person is representative of the identity, how the individual sees himself. Most people will draw a person, even if only a stick person, but some will draw robots, or monsters, the devil, just a head, and all sorts of variations. It's quite refreshing when they draw someone that is recognisable as a whole person. People with disabilities frequently draw the person with a disability, one arm or leg longer than the other, or something similar (see figure 5). Some will draw a person of the opposite gender from themselves. Others will draw only a head, and this is taken to mean that they are denying the impact of their body. In my experience, these are mostly offenders who don't want to associate with what they have done.

The three drawings are then looked at together to see if they look like a set. Usually they do but sometimes they are very different, in size, in pressure of the pencil, in style. If they are, the difference has meaning. So, for example, the person who draws a stable looking house and a strong upright tree with a healthy top, and then draws a tiny insignificant person (figure 6) will be showing that he had a good start in life, with basic emotional security and potential for ego development recognised, but then something happened to make him feel small and unimportant. This would point to something traumatic happening later in life, after initial development. This may be abuse of some kind, or having to leave home, but will be something that has caused distress and will become the focus of therapy.

Some very anxious people will draw all three pictures with very shady lines, going over and over them. Some autistic people will draw with very dark lines and very stark pictures. People who are struggling to hold themselves together will draw splintered pictures, sometimes with lots of individual bricks for the house and individual leaves for the tree, then a tiny stick person with no features.

Some years ago, when I was working in a secure setting, I was able to use the test on three occasions, on an annual basis, with a large number of people with learning disabilities. It became immediately evident that the pictures were recording change over time. People who had no interventions drew the same pictures all three times. Those receiving therapy, either group or individual, showed change. It was particularly interesting that the second set sometimes looked as though the individual was deteriorating, but then it became apparent that they were facing up to their trauma and hence developing a comprehension of their trauma as they addressed it in therapy. This work could not be published because of where it was collected but it increased confidence in the test and its usefulness.

The test is useful because it gives a lot of information quickly and without the individual feeling like a failure. Most people enjoy doing it. It's useful for all ages, from young children through to very old people. It is a powerful tool and much more revealing than self-report measures. I always include it in a battery of tests for a comprehensive assessment. It is possible to identify if there has been trauma in early childhood or later, if there are ongoing gender issues, if there is serious personality disorder, if there is risk of psychosis, and much more.

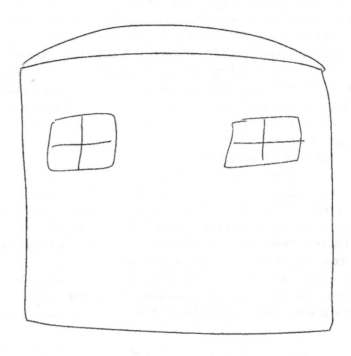

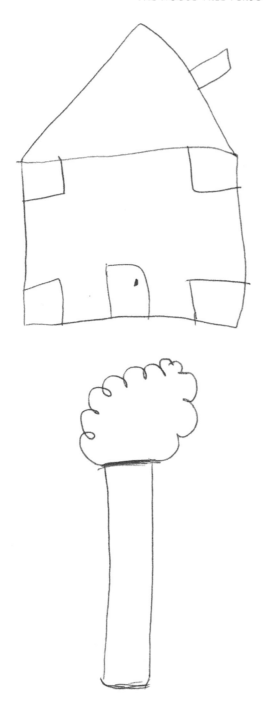

CHAPTER EIGHT

Using the object relations technique with people with intellectual disabilities

Object relations technique (ORT) is a useful theory when considering the development of the sense of self within a social framework. We develop social constructions of ourselves in relation to others. The quality of the early relationships colours all of our future relationships. It follows from this that being able to assess the quality of the early experience will assist in deciding what to do to help someone at a later stage of their life.

It is frequently the case that referrals of people with intellectual disabilities for help include an aspect of them not being able to relate to peers, or parents and support staff. There may be a litany of behaviour problems, but a clear issue will be about the level of engagement with any plans to help. This concern leads to a need to identify the difficulty and plan an intervention that might be helpful. ORT is one of the tools that can help with the identification of the problem.

ORT was developed by H Phillipson (1988) at the Tavistock Clinic. There are thirteen cards in the set, twelve with pictures on them and one blank. Individuals are asked to say what they can see in each picture, what they think is happening, and what they think will happen next. The responses are written down. For the blank card, they are asked to look at it, see if a picture comes into their head and, if so, to consider the same three points of what they can see, what is happening, and what will happen next. The test takes about twenty minutes to administer most of the time. Some people will tell long stories and they clearly take longer to record, but this doesn't happen often. When the test was first used it was with people without disabilities, and the person using the technique would question further to explore the limits of what was being said. In my experience of using it with people with disabilities, I have not done this. The main reason is because of the tendency of people with intellectual disabilities to think they must have got it wrong and then to change what they are saying. As we are trying to access the unconscious, we don't want to prompt them to think too much before they respond, so asking simple questions and recording the answer works best.

The person doing the test is exposed to only one card at a time and they are given in a particular order, which is written on the back of the cards. Once a card is finished it is turned over so as not to influence the next one. The cards are in four sets of three, one set each of one-person pictures, two-person, three-person and group. They are also in three sets of four, one set very blurred, one set with more stark black and white, and a third set with colour. The expectation is that the clearer set will produce cognitive stories, the blurred ones more imaginative stories, and the colour ones will bring out a more emotional response. The stories at each level of development will reflect the primary experience of living through that stage of development.

The one-person level is reflective of the symbiotic early relationship with the primary carer. The expectation is that most people will see the one figure in the relevant pictures and that they will be doing something benign, with a "next" of seeking contact with another.

The two-person pictures will produce stories that reflect on the two-way interaction with the primary carer, equivalent to an emotional development age of eight to fifteen months. Most people will see the two figures and the stories will give an indication of what that relationship was like for the individual.

The three-person pictures relate to the stage of development where there is the development of relationships with at least two other people, able to function in a triangular set of relationships. This is associated with Oedipal issues, competitiveness, and such like. The age equivalent would be fifteen to thirty months approximately and involve wider family relationships than the primary carer.

Group relationships are evaluated by the group pictures. The stories need to indicate that a number of figures are seen and are engaged in some level of group activity. This stage of development needs to have been achieved before school age if the individual is going to be able to function in group settings.

It is extremely useful to have an idea of the interpersonal skills of someone with an intellectual disability. It is even more useful to be able to access this information through a short and quick test which doesn't cause distress in the administration, which is generally doesn't. The exception to this is the occasional disturbance if someone is at risk of psychosis. From experience I have found that individuals with this issue will react to the first colour picture, usually rejecting it. The test is then stopped and they are reassured that it doesn't matter, something else can be considered for the assessment.

There are some common stories that are produced by people with intellectual disabilities and this probably reflects the similarity of their life experiences. It is very common for them to not be able to answer "What happens next?" and this indicates their inability to predict consequence. If people can't predict consequence they cannot use behavioural interventions that are based on cause and effect, nor can they learn from everyday experiences of cause and effect. This can be very helpful when planning a care plan, therapy, or a full package of support.

Another feature is the paucity of life and energy in the stories. They are usually very flat and with limited content. This indicates the limited access to meaningful relationships during their developmental period and a general lack of experience of relationships with others. An acknowledgement of the lack of richness can often be sufficient to enable people to think about what their life has been like so far, and to take what opportunities there are in the present and future to make up for what has been missed. These sort of flat stories give more information about what has been missing and may indicate depression or anxiety about relating to others.

There is then the group of people who have serious disturbance in their early years, often compounded by a history of disturbed behaviour. It is very often found that someone with disturbed behaviour at age thirty, has records showing that it goes back to pre-school years, but no one has been able to grasp the meaning of the behaviour. For these individuals the stories will have themes of despair, violence, sexual identity issues, anger, loss of control and so on. The most disturbed stories will usually be in one set of one-person, two-person, three-person or group level. A study of the records, or an interview with family, will provide the information of trauma at the relevant age. Where there is no corroboration it has to be assumed, but it has been corroborated enough times to have confidence in the test to assess what it claims to assess.

The individual who has suffered a traumatic experience at the two-person level, that is, within the context of the first trusting relationship, will have extreme difficulty with trust and will seek out one-to-one interaction, not being able to cope with more complex communication. They may have a diagnosis of borderline personality disorder. It is perhaps kinder to think of them as having an emotional disability as a result of trauma in the first two years of life. They will seek out one to one but will then have to keep testing the person to see if they also will let them down.

At the three-person level, there may be more disruptive behaviour, with anger and violence used to "solve" problems. This is associated with the early striving for independence which ideally happens within the safety of trustworthy adult supervision. If there has been abandonment too soon, or cruelty and neglect, the fight response is activated. They may have a diagnosis of antisocial personality disorder or be labelled as having a behavioural disorder. What they are is a two-and-a-half-year-old in an adult body trying to make sense of the world and where they fit.

Disturbed stories at the group level indicate a failure to move away from the safety of the family into school, and may reflect being sent to school early, before the development of object permanence, or some other traumatic experience like the arrival of a sibling. These individuals are usually less complex and can respond to positive behavioural support.

This brings us to the question of what is disturbance in the stories. The first thing to check is whether or not all the figures have been seen. The second thing to check is if other figures are seen that are not there. Then each set is studied, giving priority to a set with figures missing or added, as this will have indicated the stage of concern. Indications of violence, abandonment, the hero as the opposite gender, or anything "strange" is considered to be indicative of some trauma and pathology. So, for example, a three-person picture where only two people are seen, and these two people are engaged in close physical contact, would indicate feelings of rejection. Another where the colour red is seen as blood would raise concerns about having either witnessed or been involved in a violent encounter.

There is then a need to give some feedback to the individual without saying anything that would cause distress. It is not appropriate to give detailed feedback or to go through the stories with the pictures as this would uncover buried unconscious material before they are ready to look at it. The feedback is given in terms of the level of arrested development and the expected reasons for this, for example, the test shows that something upsetting may have happened when you were about two years old and this has upset the way you trust people. It is then possible to go on and explain what is proposed to help the person with the issues. It is often the case that being understood is, in itself, therapeutic and there can be a quick reduction in anxiety.

People with intellectual disabilities often don't receive recognition of their internal emotional world. Common practice is to carry out a functional assessment and an applied behaviour analysis. These techniques can be useful but they don't access the internal processes that may be driving the behaviour.

The ORT information can be readily related to HTP and the behavioural observation covered in Chapter Seven and Chapter Four. The one-person level is equivalent to the differentiation stage, the two-person to practising and the three-person to early rapprochement, with late-rapprochement being equivalent to the group stage. The quality of the drawings of HTP and the content indicates the level of development achieved, especially the tree. It is therefore useful to carry out more than one of the assessments until confidence is acquired in the professional. In time, when this confidence is acquired, it becomes more usual to use ORT with people who have good verbal competence, HTP with those who speak less but are happy to draw, and the observation with people who are either non-verbal or too cut-off from others to be able to work collaboratively.

CHAPTER NINE

Comprehensive assessment of the individual

In this chapter, we will explore the reasons for carrying out a comprehensive assessment before deciding on the appropriate intervention. We will then consider how this might be achieved. The whole approach is person centred, attempting to engage with the individual and their surroundings, to work out how they see the world and what would make it both better, and have the potential for further improvement. This is a very dynamic approach which facilitates growth. This must be detailed for people who are responding to traumatic events in childhood. This chapter addresses the assessment of the individual. For an intervention for a traumatised person, there will be systemic issues to assess and plan for, and sometimes the trauma in others, for example parents.

First do no harm—don't repeat the trauma

Before entering into a psychotherapeutic intervention, it is important to be sure that this is the appropriate intervention to undertake. Psychotherapy is hard work, and may involve a long-term commitment as well as potential distress. People who have experienced trauma must not be further traumatised. Vicarious trauma for therapist and staff must also be considered and guarded against. For some people, psychotherapy is the treatment of choice and may be the only approach that has any possibility of success. However, caution is required before embarking on the journey and careful assessment is the starting point. We must ensure that we do not make things worse and the adage of "first do no harm" is to be remembered at all times. Sometimes it will be a therapeutic environment that is recommended and the assessment needs to inform the decision between individual, systemic or both for the intervention.

In order to be sure that it is the right action, it is necessary to consider all the components of the individual and their circumstances. This includes aspects of intellect, mental health and well-being, personality and emotional developmental status, as well as home and support networks. It is usual for people with limited intellectual capacity and trauma to have some level of support and it may be full-time support for people with more severe disabilities. All aspects of the life that is led must be taken into account.

The starting point of a detailed assessment is usually intellect and the possibility of any unusual cognitive processing which may interfere with understanding, or lead to specific issues to be addressed. This is particularly relevant for people with less severe disabilities. Some individuals who are presenting as distressed, but may have severe or profound disabilities, will not be able to undertake testing but an appraisal of their level of understanding is still needed. The most common finding, in people with mild disabilities, is a left/right brain discrepancy which may have led to problems in others perception of ability. For example, people with higher verbal than performance skills will appear to be quite able, but cannot translate their thoughts into actions, and may be perceived to be lazy. The consequence for them may then have been major criticism which, in turn, affects their sense of self. At times, there will be significant brain injury, or organic impairments that bring their own complications in memory, processing information, concentration, and such like. These factors need to be known and will usually be assessed using the Wechsler (1939) instruments, or Raven's matrices (see van den Broek et al., 1994) or vocabulary scales. Sometimes there may be more assessment using neuropsychological tests to secure a more comprehensive picture. Early trauma has an impact on intellectual development, whereas later trauma may impair the ability to use the intellect to the full.

IQ tests

The Wechsler tests include the full IQ test, called the Wechsler Adult Intelligence Scale (WAIS), and the Wechsler Abbreviated Scale of Intelligence (WASI). These are standardised tests so can be considered to give a reliable result compared with the population. However, all such standardised tests will have small numbers of people for the standardising process in the lower and upper range. They are not usually used in isolation to indicate ability in people with disabilities.

The Raven progressive matrices have a coloured matrices booklet which gives an indication of level of intellectual ability and is easy to administer, making it attractive for people who are reluctant to be tested. As people with disabilities usually have an awareness of their disability, they may be reluctant to try something that they expect to fail on. Respect for potential sensitivity in this process is essential. The Wechsler tests are restricted to use by suitably qualified people (psychologists) but the Raven can be used by others. The Raven does not give a meaningful numerical result, but an indication of ability compared with the average. The Wechsler numbers for IQ are useful indicators but cannot be used in isolation. The following assessments add to the total picture.

A gentle approach is required, so as not to further traumatise individuals who feel that they are not important and not able.

Social reasoning

The next stage is to explore ability in social reasoning. The Social Reasoning Scale from the British Ability Scales is useful in evaluating the ability to consider the implications of behaviour from a social perspective. This is a subscale so is used only to assess social reasoning, not a complete test of ability.

It is useful for people with disabilities for several reasons, but the main reason is to check out whether or not someone has learned to pass tests via rote learning, but without comprehension, and, also, to see if they have "street wisdom" without the core knowledge. It is not uncommon to find people who are angry at their disability, developing skills to hide it. They score well on social reasoning as they have honed the necessary skills to present as more able than they are. However, most people with disabilities score below the level of complex reasoning and can only consider one or two angles in a social situation, rather than the three or four that is required to function well.

Where an individual has been traumatised in a social situation, it may show through in the responses.

Self-esteem

Many people with disabilities suffer from low self-esteem. Most of their lives they will have failed to succeed in whatever they have tried and will become aware of it. If they grow up in a loving family who value them as they are, they will fare better, but will still have had the school experience of not being as good at learning as others. Some people will have developed an omnipotent defence against this and present as having high self-esteem, but this may be a "false self" as described by Winnicott. There are various measures of self-esteem and the one developed by Prof. Nigel Beail and colleagues is adapted for use with the client group (based on the Rosenberg).

Mental Health

Prof. Beail has also done extensive work in adapting the Brief Symptom Inventory (Derogatis & Melisaratos, 1983) for use with people of lower intellectual ability. This instrument gives a range of scores on mental health issues like depression, anxiety, and other symptomatology. The BSI is a widely used and standardised assessment of mental health symptomatology and gives both an idea of what is troubling the individual at the present time, as well as a score that can be used to assess, at retest, if there is improvement. There are subscales of depression, anxiety, interpersonal sensitivity, obsessive-compulsive disorder, paranoid ideation, somatisation, phobic anxiety, and a global severity index. It is then possible to use the positive symptom distress index to work out the degree of distress that is experienced in relation to the symptoms rated.

History

With all assessments, the history can provide significant information. For those individuals who can give their own account it is a very similar process to taking a history from anyone else, who may not have a disability. At times, it can be very interesting if the individual gives a report and then a family member gives a very different picture. This can often be the starting point to identifying problem areas.

A lot of people with disabilities and complex needs have had many moves and many care situations. I have noted many times that people have moved every two years, sometimes from the age of two. When studying the files, it becomes clear that they attempt to form attachments and, when they fail, they become distressed and a decision is made to move them on. If the distress of the rapprochement period at the two-year developmental stage can be progressed through there is real gain, but sadly, this rarely seems to happen. Or it happens in an institutional setting when the attachment to the place becomes stronger than the attachment to people, and dependency on the institution follows.

Of course, people with disabilities endure all the same issues as other people in relation to sibling order, parental stability, and such like. Then they have their specific disabilities on top. Often, being overtaken by a younger sibling causes great pain. Undergoing medical procedures to improve appearance gives a message of inferiority. Being taken to lots of specialists to be "fixed" gives a clear message of not being good enough. The parental response to disability is crucial (Bicknell, 1983) and help for the whole family may be required.

The emotional history is very important. We need to know if there was an effective primary attachment and, if so, if that person is still available to provide emotional support.

Bringing the information together

Once there is some clarity about the cognitive ability or complexity, with the addition of information from self-report measures, it is necessary to begin to explore the unconscious material. This is accessed through the use of projective tools. The first is HTP and the next is ORT. Full chapters on these appear earlier in this book and reference will only be made to their role in the comprehensive assessment, and not on the administration. ORT is used with people who can speak and is not suitable for people with more severe disabilities. HTP can be used by anyone who can hold a pencil and draw. The drawings may not be easily recognisable as a house, tree, and person, but they are able to be interpreted. For individuals who cannot speak or draw, the observational assessment needs to be completed to clarify the emotional developmental age.

This evidence is then supplemented by a detailed history if that is possible. It may not be if there is no family involvement or scant records. Sometimes, in these situations, it is difficult to find any history and the individual becomes almost a non-person, existing only in the present. A description of the present behaviour and lifestyle is useful, including charts of problem behaviour, medication records, and information, if available, of previous interventions. Most people who are referred for psychotherapy will have complex behaviour that has not responded to other interventions.

Case examples

Lee is a twenty-four-year-old young man living in a shared house with three other young men and two staff present in the daytime, one asleep staff at night. He seemed happy when he first moved into the house. He has no family contact and has moved on from full time education, which he accessed up the age of twenty-three. He has no problems with mobility and can engage in conversation with his peers and staff. His behaviour is causing concern in that he isolates himself for long periods and will then charge out of his room in a very angry state, causing distress and some damage to property. He has not, so far, hit any other person but has hurt himself by hitting walls and doors. He is referred for assessment.

Lee attends for assessment away from the house and seems relaxed with the process. He reacts well to the assessor and there is no sign of anger or withdrawal during the process.

The first tests to be done are the tests of intellect. He is compliant and seems to enjoy the sub-tests of the WAIS, pleased when he performs well on the performance tests. He's not so good on the verbal tests but it is not so obvious to him that he is failing. The overall scores indicate that he has lower verbal ability than performance. This leads to the first hypothesis, that some of his frustration and anger may stem from having difficulty in expressing himself.

Moving on to the social reasoning scale, which he is happy to complete, reveals a very black and white view of the world, and an opinion that the child in each story is usually in the wrong. The self-esteem measure gives a low score. A picture is beginning to emerge of a young man who struggles to think and reason, and, possibly as a consequence, gets frustrated.

The next stage is to look at mental health issues and complete the BSI. There are ten sub-scales and on most of them, he scores very low, indicating no problems. However, he scores higher for depression and interpersonal difficulties. More evidence is now available to support the hypothesis that he may be unhappy and socially anxious, and this may be exacerbated by his limited verbal ability.

So far, all of the assessments have relied on his response to questions asked. The final stage is to explore what might be going on under the surface, not available in conscious thought. HTP is administered and the three drawings analysed. All three are very small and in the top left-hand corner of the page. The first impression is of feeling small and not daring to use up more space. The house is tiny, the tree is two straight lines with a ball on top, the person is a stick man with no features. The analysis indicates insecurity, poor ego development, and very limited identity development. The emptiness and lack of energy is stark.

Because he can speak, Lee is asked to complete the ORT (see Chapter Eight for details of administration). He is able to tell brief stories for each picture. All are empty of emotion or action and all end with "don't know" for what happens next. He sees the figures in the one-person, three-person, and group pictures. In the two-person pictures he sees two animals, three people, and then one person. The implication is of difficulties in early development at the two-person stage, which is the primary relationship with the mother, or the first significant other.

Examination of the available records provides the information that Lee was taken into care as a very young child and has been in various foster placements, children's homes, and residential school all his life. He has had no reliable significant other, within which relationship he might have developed a sense of self as a good enough person. The hypothesis begins to be able to incorporate cause as well as presentation.

Putting all the information together, the assessment concludes that Lee is a young man of twenty-four, with the cognitive ability of an adolescent with low verbal ability, a very under-developed ego and sense of identity, and consequent depression and interpersonal difficulties. The cause can be seen to be the absence of good-enough parenting in his early years and an institutional response to his needs. He has had no real opportunity to work out who he is or where he fits in the world. The presenting behaviour, following from the emotional deprivation, is to withdraw and then, when no one "cares enough" to come and find him, he explodes in distress and gains the support he needs as a consequence.

The recommendation would be for individual therapy in order to provide an intense relationship similar to that of primary parenting, giving him an opportunity to find himself. A further recommendation would be for him to live in a more therapeutic environment. If he can't move to another single-person service, the existing service will need to intensify the relationships by making clear to him all the time that he has a named person who is there for him and will respond to his needs.

CHAPTER TEN

Evaluation of the impact of the systemic model of trauma-informed care

Introduction

The systemic model described so far has been in use in services I have been involved with for over ten years now, with some aspects used before that. Initial use was in an NHS assessment and treatment unit, where it was possible to establish the presence of a named support worker at all times. This type of unit tends to be the default position for distressed people when their behaviour has become more than can be managed at home with family, or in a care and support setting. It has been the witnessing of such escalations that has motivated much of the study covered in this book. Some individuals are being held in secure or semi-secure environments because their behaviour is either not understood or not tolerated. It is always difficult to maintain an attachment based programme of support in temporary settings but a start can be made, and built on when the person returns to their usual place of residence.

An early application was with a young woman in her late teens who was functioning as a very young child emotionally, although cognitively was much more able. Her behaviour was very challenging. She would attack other patients in the unit, and also staff. The outbursts looked unpredictable, appearing to come from nowhere. She had been living at home with her family and the same sort of behaviour was happening there. At times, she would withdraw completely, going to her room and closing the door. Then, some time later, she would burst out and attack whoever was nearest.

At first, it seemed as though she withdrew from contact and that she did this to rest. Then it was considered that she spent time building herself up to the next attack. Most people were very wary of her and reluctant to be anywhere near her door. This meant that she often couldn't hear if anyone was near. It began to feel more like she withdrew because she didn't know what else to do. She was not connected to anyone so was not seeking meaningful contact or engaging in activities. An observation of her led to the identification of the early rapprochement stage of development. She was not able to hold on to a sense of herself as an individuated person, but she was not able, either, to negotiate at the late rapprochement stage, for what she needed. Her attacks were seen as attempts to make contact, although, of course, they were experienced by others as hostile and very frightening.

Identifying trauma

The trauma was identified, after interviews with her parents, as a hospital experience before the age of two. Her parents were asked if they could recall any time that their daughter was distressed before the age of five. It's important to ask a general question so as not to lead the answer. In my experience, parents can always recall vividly when there has been a traumatic event, as they have been equally distressed by it. However, they rarely are able to connect it with the presenting situation, either because it is hard to believe in the long-term consequences, or they can't bear to think about it themselves. Her behaviours were in the early rapprochement stage, the stage she would have been at when the traumatic visit to hospital happened. The failure to develop from then was probably missed because of her learning disability. As she failed to develop skills, it was thought that it was because she couldn't. It was not common for professionals to be alert to attachment and emotional problems in young children. She continued to grow and to learn what she could, but to always be unsettled if she wasn't in close contact with someone she knew and trusted. As this led to conflict at home when she was more demanding of her mother's time, she was provided with more respite care. This, of course, led to more attachment problems.

She needed lots of two-way interaction that was positive and developmental if she was to be helped. A named individual member of staff was made available for her all the time. She was given a chart in her room with pictures of all the staff and the relevant significant other was placed on the chart for the hours they would be there. This meant that she always knew, every minute of the day, who was going to be there for her. At night, she was told and shown who would be there when she woke in the morning or during the night. The reduction in anxiety was almost instant.

She quickly responded to the availability of another person to test out her reactions and interactions, becoming very emotionally draining for staff in the short term, but then settling to a more negotiation type style. Suitable activities were planned and provided, from making sure that mealtimes were a pleasant two-person activity, to walks and games involving just her and her named member of staff. She became a pleasure to be with and developed skills with games and activities that had previously needed a lot of support. As she became more competent and relaxed, she began to move through the rapprochement stage and to want to be more directive, choosing rather than responding. This is appropriate to the continuation through from early to late rapprochement. It does require that the attachment figure is able to celebrate the developing independence, and be able to accept a level of risk, thus facilitating exploring and experimentation.

Staff

Unfortunately, staff were less tolerant of her growing independence and were not able to help her through this next stage. During early rapprochement she had been fun to be with, always keen to be with her named person, giving them clarity of role and direction for their shift. As she became more confident and seeking to negotiate, it became more of a challenge for the staff. The difficult attacking behaviour had gone, so, to some extent, their work was done. It was hard to help them to see that the more the young woman could choose and direct her own life, the better it was for her. This raised for me the suitability of assessment and treatment units for this type of work. It is perhaps better to put the plan in place in the community setting that is going to be the long term home. Issues of advocacy and choice are huge. The process of letting go is hard for care and support staff. It is also quite difficult when the behaviour has been seen as stuck for many years. It is quite usual for professionals to believe that some challenging behaviour cannot change when there has been no response to medication, an environmental manipulation, or a behaviour programme.

I began to focus my thinking on what is needed to enable staff to provide the necessary nurturing environment. This is needed for individuals to thrive and grow emotionally. Staff are generally quite good at skill development and pursuit of leisure opportunities, but the finer tuning required to meet the people they support as traumatised human beings is much harder. For some the impact of the trauma is too much. Some events don't bear thinking about and have the impact of blocking the thinking of the carers. This is a counter-transference phenomenon that is reported by Bion (1963) where carers become unable to process information that is either too distressing, or shut off by the person being supported because of the depth of trauma. The presence of this sort of distancing can be used diagnostically to establish the presence of traumatic life events in early life.

Training and support

So the first stage of evaluation led to the identification of the need for training and support for staff to provide the model, before it could be properly evaluated. A training course called "All behaviour has meaning" was designed first. This looked at behavioural, cognitive, psychodynamic, and systems approaches to understanding behaviour. Staff were asked to keep in mind a particular client and relate what they were learning to that client. They were asked to think of interventions in each area that matched what they observed in the client. At the end, they were asked to consider the approach that most closely matched the identified need in the client. This enables people to be more person centred in the approach and to see that more than one type of work can have an impact. It is the matching that is important. They were also helped to see that behavioural and cognitive techniques have limited impact if the person is pre-individuation developmentally.

Once the intervention is in place, it is necessary to provide ongoing support for staff groups. They need to be helped to change the way they behave with the client as development occurs, or they will inadvertently stop it happening. They may need help usually, to deal with their own feelings in response to the traumatic events of the individual they are supporting.

Is it possible?

Consideration of the possibility that it is not possible was also taken. My own understanding had come from many years of work in the field and an extended period of study. It has sometimes been the case that an approach works if delivered by the main proposer, but is not replicable by others. There is research to show that some techniques work better if delivered by psychologists than other staff. If this approach needs qualified psychologists to work full time with clients, then it is doomed to failure as too expensive and not appropriate. The challenge was, therefore, to see if it could be put in place successfully when provided by staff who had been trained but didn't necessarily have a full understanding.

The following is a description of another intervention and the thinking processes. It is presented in a format that anonymises the individual as much as possible.

Putting it into practice

Summary

There is much focus on behavioural interventions used with people with intellectual disabilities and challenging behaviours, but there is limited literature outlining the use of interventions informed by emotional developmental models linked to early trauma for these individuals. This case study outlines the application of an intervention based on an emotional development framework developed by me (Frankish, 1989, 1992, 2013a) for use with people with intellectual disabilities experiencing emotional disturbance displayed in their behaviour. We are thinking of people with severe intellectual disabilities and a history of highly distressed behaviour, occasionally requiring restraint, who experienced both physical and emotional trauma as a baby. They can live with the right support in the community. The staff team need introductory training in emotional development and regular psychology consultancy. The individual's stage of emotional development is assessed over the project, and qualitative information from the case notes and discussions with the staff are considered to provide context. It has been found that the individual's emotional development progresses from early to later phases. Distressed behaviour is reported to reduce in intensity, and assaults on staff were much less frequent. Findings so far suggest that emotional development can occur in individuals whose development has previously been arrested and/or regressed, when their staff team is provided with training and regular psychology consultancy relating to the emotional development of the individual. This emotional development enables individuals to have a greater ability to contain their own distress, and engage with others, than if the development had not occurred.

Introduction to this individual situation

Historically, people with intellectual disabilities and challenging behaviour have lived in large institutions separated from the rest of their communities and the focus of intervention was to eliminate or physically contain their behaviour, often with minimal understanding of its causes and meaning. With the closure of institutions in favour of support in the community, there has been greater focus on understanding the meaning and function of the behaviour and providing interventions to manage the behaviour based on this understanding (Emerson, 2001; Osgood, 2004). Positive behavioural support has taken the behavioural model forward to provide more comprehensive, specialised packages of care for people displaying such difficulties.

With the closure of the institutions, individuals whose behaviour challenged their community placement, resulting in placement breakdown, have usually been provided with care in hospitals or specialist units with varying levels of security. Without suitable care packages providing appropriate levels of support in the community being commissioned, these individuals can remain in hospital settings for years, where their opportunities for an ordinary home life are greatly minimised. For these individuals, wherever they live, it is important that their care package is developed with the individual in mind and that their staff are appropriately skilled and trained and have access to professional advice to support the implementation of interventions facilitating positive behavioural change (Perry, Felce, Allen, & Meek, 2011).

There has been developing understanding of the need to consider the emotional lives of people with intellectual disabilities and challenging behaviour (Frankish, 2013). Psychological therapies are recognised as valid and effective ways of supporting these individuals (Beail, 1998, 2001; Berry, 2003; Parkes et al., 2007; Rhodes et al., 2011; Sinason, 2010).

I recognised in people with severe intellectual disabilities and challenging behaviour, the same type of behaviours as described by Mahler (1975) referring to the phases from total dependence to independence in children. This, she suggested, indicated that the individuals were emotionally developmentally delayed and the point at which they were delayed could be measured using Mahler's phases (differentiation, practising, early and late rapprochement). From this I developed an observational assessment (Frankish, 2013a) of the emotional developmental level of individuals with intellectual disabilities, to ascertain the nature and quality of interpersonal support they required to continue in their emotional development (see Chapter Six). This is particularly pertinent for individuals whose emotional development has been arrested as a result of trauma and as such have not reached their potential.

Frankish's (2013a) observational assessment of the emotional developmental level of individuals with severe intellectual disabilities led to the allocation of a developmental phase that was consistent between observers. Once this stage has been identified, the correct level of emotional support can be provided, facilitating more development. Further observation later establishes whether or not progress has been made.

This case study explores the application of this emotional developmental perspective to support people with severe intellectual disabilities and challenging behaviour whose emotional development was arrested following trauma in babyhood. It utilises the observational tool to monitor individuals' emotional development following moves from assessment and treatment units in a hospital to specialist tenancies in the community. We have found that behaviour that had not significantly changed for many years despite living in different environments does change when the emotional developmental approach is used and emotional needs are met.

Examples of similar cases

During time in hospital, some people exhibit very distressed behaviour, including physical aggression to others and self-injurious behaviour, occasionally causing serious injury. This behaviour is usually managed with high levels of medication, above recommended limits, and with control and restraint procedures involving up to five members of staff. There are usually waking night staff available. Often they are not able to share living space and become intolerant of eye contact and touch.

Due to pressures from government initiatives, moves to live in services provided in the community have become the norm. Some live in a single person's service supported by staff twenty-four hours a day. The interior of properties can be designed for specific use, and, in time, they can share with others. Properties may need a room (a safe room) designed to keep individuals safe when distress is severe enough that it cannot be contained. This room needs a stable-style door, so that when closed it is still possible to see out, participate, interact, and observe. This is considered a less restrictive alternative to a five-person restraint which has often been considered to be necessary in the past.

Following assessment of an individual's emotional development using the observational assessment, the staff team are provided with training and consultation sessions to help them provide care appropriate to the level of emotional development. The staff team are also provided with a more general training about disability psychotherapy to give them a broader understanding of the model. The training provides an introduction to psychoanalytical theories, emotional development, attachment theory, and psychodynamic perspectives, with particular emphasis on Winnicott (1973) and Bowlby. It also provides an introduction to carrying out the observational assessment of emotional development. The training and the consultation aim to enable the staff teams to provide a secure base for the person they support with the knowledge of their particular emotional developmental needs and how best to support them with this understanding in mind.

To evaluate any changes in the emotional development, people are assessed each year using the observational assessment. These show if progress is being made, and evidence to date shows that individuals make progress through the phases. Along with these assessments, records are reviewed to provide a context to the period under consideration and qualitative information of changes or notable events.

The staff monitor behaviour daily at regular intervals throughout the waking hours and keep file notes and incident forms. This information is used to identify any significant behavioural, personal, and environmental changes that occur across the duration of the care plan.

Results so far with the approach

When looking through reports of people for whom this approach has been found to be useful, it becomes clear that initially the individuals have major trauma in their past, severe behavioural disturbance in the present and are usually functioning at the emotional developmental level of twelve to eighteen months. This corresponds to the practising level in the phase model and represents a need for reliable and constant emotional support. Later reports show moves into early rapprochement and better quality of life as a consequence of more interaction.

The behavioural records and notes also show a number of changes. The incidents of physical aggression to staff reduce steadily over time. An example would be of someone who, before they first moved had over fifty incidents of this nature in a three-month period, a year later had just under twenty, and for the next two years reduced to a handful of such incidents with many months with no such incidents at all.

The staff record when an individual is "unsettled", which is when they are agitated, for example showing aggression to staff (without contact), screaming, or initiating self-injurious behaviour. If this behaviour and distress escalates then they would be directed, first orally and then by escort if necessary to the "safe room" where they would be safe to de-escalate with visual and auditory contact with support staff. The staff's monitoring identifies if they continue to show unsettled behaviour to a greater or lesser degree, and this can be still to a high level (sometimes more than 100 incidents recorded in a three-month period). However, the use of the safe room reduces over time from more than 80 incidents in three months during the first year of a care plan to 10 in the most recent period for one individual.

The staffing levels in one example have reduced from a ratio of three to one, to one to one with backup, and one to one at night. Sometimes individuals remain on a high level of medication (but within recommended limits) and this is kept under regular review. Sharing the home with other individuals with intellectual disabilities becomes possible. They become able to initiate social interaction with staff and peers and to tolerate eye contact for short periods without distress. They usually continue to prefer others to respect their own space and so personal areas are not accessed unless necessary.

What does it mean for the future?

Using the observational tool of emotional development, this work shows that the level of emotional development can progress from the differentiation/practising phases to the early rapprochement phase over the course of the study. This development has occurred in the context of the staff having received introductory training in disability psychotherapy and psychology consultancy on a regular basis to implement their learning about the people they support.

Records show that physical aggression towards staff reduces considerably and despite continued high levels of unsettled/distressed behaviour (including attempted physical aggression and self-injurious behaviour) the use of the safe room reduces. This indicates that distress may not reduce in frequency, but reduces in intensity and people become better able to contain their distress without the need for the safe room. The records also highlight the reduction in staffing required to support, the development of the ability to share (some of) the space, and the development of social skills. These findings also support the observational assessment analysis that progress is made to the early rapprochement phase where social interaction is developing as the individual continues to move from dependency to independence.

This tells the story of the use of this emotional developmental perspective with a few individuals with intellectual disabilities and challenging behaviour. Therefore, it is necessary to be cautious in applying the findings more widely. Further research is required on a larger scale to add to this and previous research (Frankish, 1989, 2013). However, it looks promising and has a simplicity to it that should make it more attractive to other service providers.

The key elements are person-centred care and support, with the assessment of the needs of the individual being supported including a measure of their emotional development. Many behavioural and cognitive assessments start from an assumption that the individual has reached a stage of knowing who they are. These very distressed individuals have not developed a reliable sense of self. Having the opportunity to do this, within the context of a secure, emotionally supportive environment, leads to change and improved quality of life.

Reflections on the case study approach

This complex care package was provided for a severely disabled person in order to create a therapeutic environment; it has led to her progressing from the practising stage of emotional development through to the early rapprochement stage. Care plan data has been routinely collected so this has not been a research project, more an evaluation of a care plan.

Data collected has included information on levels of medication taken and incidents of disturbed behaviour requiring intervention. There is a continuous record over daytime hours, at half-hourly intervals, of aspects of behaviour that indicate both positive and negative aspects. These have included activities as well as being unsettled, settled, engaged with staff, agitated and such like. From this data, it has been possible to chart changes over time, indicating an increase in positive behaviour and a decrease in negative behaviour. This individual is now settled for much of the time. Prior to the move into the emotionally nurturing setting, the picture was very different.

A further consequence of the intervention has been a reduction in the level of staff support that is needed. As relating to staff has improved, it has become evident that the individual can tolerate better the joint activities that are necessary, like personal care, dressing and eating. One-to-one support is now sufficient much of the time, with someone else available at critical times like bathing and dressing. This is a significant reduction.

Prior to the move it was very common for aggressive outbursts to happen, including damage to self, others, and property. These have all reduced. Damage to property is not commented on and damage is repaired as quickly as possible. There are no incidents when "the man" comes in to fix the hole in the wall, as if it is understood that mending things puts them right. Harm to self and others is occasionally threatened now but is managed by asking the individual to go into a soft play area where they can listen to music and calm down without risk of self-harm. This is responded to well and communication continues throughout the calming period. There are often tears at the end of a disturbed period, which seems to be a recognition of the intensity of feeling.

Pressures on staff

This type of approach is very demanding of staff and staff support sessions are made available to address this. Staff react to the projections from traumatised people and become distressed or angry themselves. They can, at times, lose sight of the needs of the person they are supporting, as they become more involved in their own. In the support sessions they are encouraged to air their thoughts and feelings, check out with each other how they are feeling, and look for some processing of the distress and trauma in the session. If they can succeed in doing this, they will be more able to withstand the projections the next time. Of course, more issues arise and the process is ongoing.

It is particularly hard to enable someone to progress through the rapprochement stage, as this requires meaningful two-person interactions. At the earlier stages the parent-child model works fairly well because the need for emotional security is paramount. At the rapprochement stage, the adult needs to gradually reduce the level of guidance to permit development and growth, while at the same time, making judgements about the level so as not to leave the individual feeling abandoned.

CHAPTER ELEVEN

Evaluation of the impact of individual psychotherapy

This chapter will consider the difference between individual psychotherapy for people without intellectual disability, and disability psychotherapy. There are many similarities but also some differences that are crucial for the success of the therapy.

Both address the internal world. Individual psychotherapy developed from the work of Freud and the acceptance of the existence of the unconscious. The question addressed here is about how we access the unconscious, especially with people who may not speak, bearing in mind that psychotherapy is referred to as a talking therapy. There is still considerable dispute about the effectiveness of psychotherapy but a report by Roth and Fonagy (2005) has provided evidence of effectiveness. As the treatment approach is very individual, it doesn't lend itself to clinical trials, and this will always be a handicap in securing full recognition. Self-report by people who have had therapy is generally very positive. The range of therapy approaches is probably as wide as the number of therapists, as it is essential that the therapist be a person and not just a professional in the encounter.

It is worth mentioning here the work of Carl Rogers (1951) and person-centred therapy. All therapy needs to be person centred but there can be a tendency to rely on techniques and to lose the person in the process. People with intellectual disability are very quick to feel the "absence" of the therapist if their attention wavers or if they are not wholly committed to the endeavour. Rogers and others speak about unconditional regard for the other as a core requirement. This unconditional regard is what babies and small children need if they are to develop and grow. The therapy is therefore providing a reparative experience, to compensate for what may have not been good enough in early life, giving a sounding board for the person to explore their feelings. The safety of the relationship is vital to this process.

There are now many therapeutic approaches with a variety of names. Mindfulness has come to the fore in the early twenty-first century (Gilbert, 2010). It is an approach that encourages the individual to be mindful of themselves, to look inside at their feelings and reactions to others, to then develop compassion towards themselves and others, leading to inner peace and reduction in anxiety. Solution-focused therapy combines cognitive and emotional responses to problems and helps with the development of personal techniques that assist with the management of internal distress. Others focus on the body's reaction to distress, using physiological responses to help to increase awareness of issues that are problematic. There are many more and all have their place. They are all based on the primary presumption that internal processes affect external behaviour. Most will be examining life events that have caused stress or trauma that need to be processed.

Disability psychotherapy focuses on early emotional development, with or without later trauma. Experience has shown that people with intellectual disabilities have frequently been traumatised several times, and their early trauma, pre-individuation, has interfered with their ability to withstand later traumatic events. There is a qualitative difference between people who have individuated and then experienced trauma, and those who have suffered traumatic experiences at a younger age, before they have an individuated sense of self. Some people with intellectual disabilities will be individuated and have had later traumatic life experiences. They will respond to therapy in a very similar way to individuals without disability. They are often able to be treated quite quickly with cognitive approaches. Quite quickly means months rather than years. Psychodynamic psychotherapy for people traumatised in early life does take years, as it is a growth process based on the establishment of an attachment figure (the therapist) and working through of past trauma.

There is still a limited evidence base for the effectiveness of disability psychotherapy. However, Beail has published some evidence, as has Alim, and there is an old paper of mine (Frankish, 1989) which shows change over time and the effectiveness of the stage model of development as being a useful way to evaluate effectiveness. Beail, with colleagues, has examined the impact of therapy and the process. A significant issue is around acceptance of offending behaviour, which can be a major problem for people who are still effectively two years old in an adult body and a survivor of abuse. Their behaviour can be a re-working of the abuse. Owning the source of the pain is a big step. In his 2013 paper, "From denial to acceptance of sexually offending behaviour: a psychodynamic approach", Beail is able to show that this is possible and forms the foundation of further work towards a more ordinary life. Beail uses the concepts of assimilation of problematic experience to chart the progress through therapy. In the early stages they are "warded off", denying responsibility for or awareness of their behaviour. This moves through levels to the point of acceptance and a willingness to address both the problematic behaviour and the sense of self as a good-enough person.

Alim (2010) looks at the usefulness of the Malan (2001) approach and progress through therapy. Beail had shown that people move through the stages of assimilation, and this is replicated in Alim's study.

Frankish (1989) used the observational method to establish the emotional developmental stage, provided individual therapy, and re-measured. All showed progress through the stages, and it was notable that the younger the client, the more progress was made. The sample was too small for any hard conclusions but the inference is that early intervention works quicker, implying that people become stuck in their non-adaptive way of relating and it is then harder to change.

I have continued to see people for individual therapy and to evaluate the effectiveness using the methods covered in previous chapters, but also adding the Brief Symptom Inventory. This is widely used and recognised as a useful measure of mental wellbeing or illness. Beail and Frankish established some norms for people with ID some years ago and these are useful. We found that there were more reported symptoms relating to personality than to mental illness in our sample, and this concurs with the theory of emotional disability as a result of impaired early experience. Others might call this an attachment disorder, and this would not be inappropriate. It is, however, easier to put together a reparative therapy plan based on stage-related behaviour and clear goals. Many people who have had inadequate attachment experiences will not have the capacity to form good attachments, so respond better to a plan that is aiming to progress their development, rather than one that emphasises what they haven't got and can't have.

In my experience of individual work and supervising others, I have seen dramatic improvements in a short time once the right therapeutic environment is provided, both individually and in the living space. I have also seen people for up to eight years of individual therapy. These longer therapies go through stages themselves that map on to the developmental stages. The early work is about making a connection and being reliable even though there is little positive feedback from the client. This is very like being a reliable other to a young child. This may be followed by some acting out (practising behaviour), then some testing (early rapprochement), moving on to joint working on the issues of past trauma with the associated pain and distress. It follows that, from the outside, people can be seen to get worse before they get better. This can show in HTP as well, where developing awareness can show as disintegration or depression. It is important to keep going at this point, or the work will not only be wasted, but could result in more trauma, from the perception of being abandoned again. As professionals, we are sometimes left in a difficult position if others are saying the therapy must stop, or someone leaves their job. There is an ethical position to maintain when putting a case to continue. Similarly, we shouldn't take on long-term work if we know we may leave the job. Honesty is an essential ingredient to effective therapy, especially for people with early trauma who lack the robustness that comes with the established sense of self.

When evaluating the impact of disability psychotherapy we are usually looking at quality of life issues. There may be test results that show progress as well, which is always useful to show others and to justify the work. The main factors, however, take us back to O'Brien's five principles of an ordinary life (in Brown & Benson, 1992). These are community presence, relationships, choice, competence, and respect. I will address each of these.

Community presence is a therapeutic outcome that I have witnessed many times. People offered therapy in secure settings, manage to move on to community placements. People in residential care settings move on to supported living. I think of examples of individuals who have been stuck in the same place for many years, with everyone saying they can't change, who, when offered a real human therapeutic relationship, respond and grow a sense of themselves that they can take into ordinary settings. Other examples are of people being able to function with lower staffing levels.

Relationships prosper once one good-enough relationship has been made. Once one person can be trusted, it becomes possible to trust another person. This is moving from the two-person level of relating, to the three-person level. It usually goes to a second two-person relationship first, and then the increased confidence leads to others being "seen" as potential friends, or at least acquaintances. Sometimes the first sign of this will be an individual asking for something instead of waiting passively for things to be given. You have to trust that it will be given before you ask, and this can be a major breakthrough.

Choice is another big issue. People who are traumatised and have arrested emotional development cannot make choices. This is particularly noticeable with people with autism, a condition that presents as delayed emotional development. Asking them to choose creates major anxiety. Fear of making the wrong choice is huge. This seems to link to fear of losing the thing not chosen. The ability to choose and accept the loss comes with the tolerance of uncertainty that is not available until there is a sense of self that is secure, So helping people to acquire the skills to choose comes into the therapeutic work. Initially choice is not given, because it is too stressful. This can look oppressive and it is important to make sure other colleagues, families, and staff where relevant, know why choice is being limited. An outcome of therapy is the ability to choose. We can only choose if we value what is on offer, and this comes from knowing, which in turn, comes from being aware. These are all stages of development that ideally are traversed in early childhood.

Competence, and the right to show what you can do, is often denied to people with intellectual disability. They are so often told what they are doing, where they are going, and treated as if they cannot do things for themselves. It is often quicker to cook a meal for someone instead of taking the time to help them to do it themselves, and then learn to do it themselves in future. Some of the most distressed people who come for therapy are also the most competent, but don't use their skills. This is often because of behaviour problems that lead to them being denied access to ordinary living. Once they have progressed to the rapprochement stage, they can usually interact with others and learn new skills, becoming able to celebrate what they have achieved.

Perhaps the most important is respect. Everyone has the right to be respected. Therapy that starts from a position of equality is respectful. Therapies that are very directive are using an expert-learner model. Psychotherapy starts from a position of two people in a room for the benefit of one of them, and then goes where it goes. The emphasis is on the relationship in the room. Respect is given for everything the individual brings. This enables them to trust and to share their thoughts and feelings about what has happened to them.

Individual psychotherapy can be evaluated by test results and these have consistently shown improvement over time. There is not much published data but what there is, is positive. My own early results have been replicated many times and more results are in preparation for publication (e.g., Larson et al., 2011).

Perhaps the more important evaluation is about quality of life. The individuals who reach the accomplishments that O'Brien speaks about will have a better quality of life. They will be visible, engaged, and listened to, with the needs that come from their disability met, and their rights as a human being acknowledged.

CHAPTER TWELVE

Comparison with other therapeutic models

Cognitive behaviour therapies

Models used with people without intellectual disabilities have mostly been adapted for use with this client group from work with non-disabled people. Cognitive behaviour therapy (CBT), in particular, has been used quite widely with people with less severe intellectual disabilities and especially with forensic populations for anger management and sexual offending. Taylor (2002) and Lindsay (1994, 1996, 2006) have been prolific in publishing data on the effectiveness of these approaches (see below). A lot of this work has been group-work. The recognition of early attachment problems is recognised but not always worked with directly. The intervention is at a cognitive level, while giving support for the need to encourage trust and trusting relationships. As there is no reported measure of emotional developmental stage, it is not possible to make a direct comparison but the expectation would be that the interventions that are effective are with people who are at least at the late rapprochement stage of development. The ability to learn, which is necessary for cognitive work, only comes with an internal state of knowing the self and being able to build on what is known.

Within CBT, there is a range of other therapies. Solution-focused therapy and problem-solving techniques can be helpful with verbal, mildly disabled people. They require a degree of engagement with the process and an ability to absorb knowledge. Similarly with mindfulness; an approach that teaches people to live in the present and to be aware of their own reactions to things around them. Compassion-focused therapy using mindfulness is growing in popularity with non-disabled people and long-term mental health patients. It aims to assist with self-care as well as awareness of the needs of others, once the recognition of their own pain is accepted and lived with. Most of these approaches have whole books and manuals in their own right and are mentioned here to acknowledge the range of options that are there for people. It is a source of interest generally that more approaches are developed but all spring from the same core base, that of learning to live with what cannot be changed. In the disability world there is so much that cannot be changed and the therapeutic approaches must always be brave enough to face that fact.

Treatment for offenders

A number of prescribed treatments have been designed and developed and these can be usefully applied in a variety of settings. John Taylor has been delivering anger management programmes in a secure setting for some years with positive results. This programme, described by Willner et al. (2013), produced good results in reductions in anger and challenging behaviour, as reported by individuals, staff and families. The work is group therapy using CBT and is hospital based. The researchers set out to evaluate the effectiveness of the group work with 179 people with learning disabilities. Half received therapy and half didn't, acting as a control group. The pre-therapy assessment included self-report measures of how the participants would respond to hypothetical and real anger-provoking situations. The results showed that there was a significant reduction in anger responses to real situations and all benefitted from the experience of the work.

Similarly, Lindsay (2006) has provided treatments for sexual offending and found a 70% harm reduction, identifying that appropriate social engagement and treatment are both needed to achieve good results.

Group work for sexual knowledge and for sexual offending was established by Murphy in the 1980s and continues to deliver results using CBT. Reduced offending is noted as well as some deeper understanding of what processes are involved. Finkelhor (1984) established that there are four pre-conditions to sexual offending and these are addressed in the therapy. They are: motivation to offend (often based on past experience); overcoming internal inhibitors; overcoming external obstacles (e.g., find a place); and overcoming victim resistance (perhaps by befriending).

Murphy also found that there was a pattern of insecure attachment leading to low self-esteem, with the potential for hostility if rejected or the seeking of pleasure as consolation. From this model of understanding, it has been possible to plan interventions that address all the components, with good results.

Psychoanalytic therapy

Respond, in central London, a charity set up to provide therapy from a psychoanalytic understanding that has been in existence since 1991, reports good outcomes from its work. The charity was set up to "lessen the effect of trauma and abuse on people with learning disabilities, their families and supporters".

The Respond model is based on attachment theory, object relations, developmental theories, and systemic theory, and so is very similar to the Frankish model. We are both beginning to benefit from recent research into the impact of trauma on brain development. We have been able to see, for many years, that there is arrested emotional development and the neuroscience that is now showing that the brain does not develop in the same way when trauma in early childhood is present, is proving useful. The therapeutic work does help people to change and it would be worthwhile to see if the brain does respond physiologically, or if another part of the brain takes over the function. All of the work at Respond is outpatient work.

Respond has also been involved in furthering the work of bereavement counselling. Noelle Blackman (2003) has offered a group experience for people with learning disabilities whose response to loss is not always acknowledged or tolerated. It has been my experience, too, to find that there is an assumption that people of lesser intellectual ability will respond differently to grief. They do, of course, have the same issues as anyone else and have, in addition, their own pain about what they have lost because of their disability. This is valuable work and has been replicated in other places and is a service that is now accepted as a right. As people with disabilities are living longer, they will experience more losses, of parents, maybe siblings, and care staff. These extra losses need to be faced and ways found to keep going, the same as they are needed for anyone else.

Prof. Nigel Beail has been working in Barnsley for many years and has also trained lots of other people to provide individual therapy using psychoanalytic techniques and evaluating the therapy using Malan's approach. By doing this, he has been able to publish some outcome data to indicate both the impact and also the process of therapy. This informs the debate about effectiveness and cost. It has been generally accepted that psychoanalytic-based therapy will always be long term and the consequent cost has been viewed negatively. There is a similar issue with the necessary training to be able to deliver such therapy. To date there are no recognised trainings aimed at this client group although we are trying to establish a course locally. The Institute of Psychotherapy and Disability (IPD) was formed with the aim of making progress in this area and continues to be a forum for discussion, sharing, and developing trainings. The right to have access to the therapy that is needed is still not met and probably won't be for many years.

Pre-therapy

Gary Prouty (1994) put forward a view that there is something called pre-therapy that prepares people with intellectual disabilities for cognitive work. This is based on the need to help the individual to engage with the process, to trust that the therapist wants to help, and to reach a level of emotional maturity that allows for two-way interaction. From the perspective of this book, pre-therapy would be therapy, in most cases. However, the term pre-therapy has proved useful and is not discounted. It is good that there is recognition of the need for engagement before the specific therapeutic intervention can be likely to succeed.

Intensive interaction

Another approach that has some similarities is intensive interaction (Firth et al., 2008). The aim here is to work in very close proximity to the individual and to work towards a level of attunement so that the distressed individual feels the contact of the other person. This is almost replicating the initial mother-child experience and leads to the development of interest in the other person. It is of most benefit for people who are at the symbiotic or differentiation level of emotional development. When the client is able to feel the presence of the other, they become able to respond and to value that presence. Most people who benefit from this approach are profoundly or multiply disabled, and pre-verbal. Sessions are frequent and enjoyable, giving a positive experience for everyone together with genuine warmth and unconditional regard. The main difference from the approach expounded here is in the sessional nature of the work. I have found that providing the significant other at all times, and adding the more intense sessions, provides a continuity that reduces anxiety significantly and consequently reduces problematic behaviours like self-harm in the form of attacks on the body.

Similarities and differences

It can be argued that all approaches have value and that is not denied. Matching the therapy and therapist to the client is very often a key matter. This is particularly true of individual therapy. It makes it difficult to gather enough data that will support a contention that the work is both effective, efficacious, and value for money. It was the pressure of the system to deliver cost-effective and sound interventions that led to much of the development covered by this book. Individual therapy for all is never going to be funded. Approaches that use the ideas, and provide a way of offering help that is cost-effective, progressive, and understood by non-specialist staff, are essential. This is not to decry the masses of good work that is happening across the world on an individual basis. It is to add to what is on offer in the hope that more people will have rewarding emotional experiences that allow them to grow emotionally and enjoy more of what ordinary life has to offer, free of some of the extreme anxiety that many of them experience.

The similarities lie in the foundation stones. All of the therapies are based on recognition of the impact of life experience, especially trauma. Some look at very primary processes, some at later events. Some consider internal dialogue and others concentrate more on emotions without words. The essential nature of my approach is that it is holistic and person centred, taking into account all aspects of life. Most of the referrals are people who have no secure base for daily living, finances, or support, and have such a fragile sense of self that they can't solve their problems themselves. Some have serious intellectual impairments and some have autism. Some are more intellectually able but have serious emotional trauma. All are very individual and the intervention package must allow for this. It causes difficulties sometimes when people ask to see where the service is going to be as there is no "service" to look at. Each package is designed around the individual and varies according to the level and type of need.

All therapy is a growth experience, designed to assist individuals to be more resilient and able to cope with life. For the complex traumatised individuals that we meet it is a long road. But it is a road that can be travelled in the community. It doesn't have to be travelled in locked accommodation cut off from ordinary life. It may cost nearly as much but the potential for longer-term reductions as improvement is achieved is there. When I think about my early days in the long-stay institutions and the people who did not change for year on year, I know that this must never happen again. Providing a therapeutic intervention that meets the emotional, intellectual, and physical needs of the distressed individual is possible, essential, and a human right.

CHAPTER THIRTEEN

Future use of the model

Résumé

When I refer to "the model", I am talking about the model of working with the emotional needs of people with intellectual disabilities. This is from all angles, the assessment and recognition of the emotional world of people who have traditionally been neglected in this area. Also, I am looking at the interventions that are needed to address the issues, the therapy, the secure base, and support for staff and carers.

At the time of writing, we are in a climate of political change, and over the past few years there has been a willingness to consider emotional needs in response to cruelty in secure settings. The report on the Winterbourne View hospital, and its closure, raised the issues into national awareness. Much was said about how wrong it was, but there has been little done to change it. Norman Lamb, the relevant government minister at the time, has led a piece of work and come up with recommendations. Hopefully these will be put into practice and make a difference. The necessary resources are probably there if they are deployed well enough.

A consultation document from the Department of Health, *No Voice Unheard, No Right Ignored—A Consultation for People with Learning*

Disabilities, Autism and Mental Health Conditions, was circulated in spring 2015 with responses asked for by May.

The scope of the consultation primarily related to assessment and treatment in mental health hospitals for people (all ages) with learning disability or autism; adult care and support, primarily for those with learning disability but also for adults with autism (and the links to support for children and young people); and all those to whom the Mental Health Act currently applies (including children and young people). Other elements were included, particularly where they relate to the Care Act 2014, that may be of relevance to adults in receipt of social care, including those with other disabilities.

Some of the proposals related to possible amendments to the Mental Health Act, which were not intended to apply to patients under Part III of the Mental Health Act (those who have entered via the criminal justice system). This is because of those patients' particular needs and the important responsibility of the Secretary of State for Justice and the National Offender Management Service in relation to public protection. The scope of proposals in relation to this group of patients was set out for each relevant section.

At the time of writing, the consultation is still in process. This document is considering the practicalities of making sure that no one is unheard and abused while in receipt of services for treatment and care. It has echoes of the hospital enquiries of the 1970s and the book *Hospitals in Trouble* (Martin & Evans, 1984) comes to mind. It is clear that there have been many attempts over the years to provide protection and a voice for people with disabilities and significant progress has been made. However, very complex people, who have emotional issues and complex needs as well as their intellectual or other disability, are still in need of a planned approach. What is put forward here is just such an approach. If everyone who was deemed to have complex needs received the same approach, there would be no room for the failures that have been evident over many years.

I will summarise the elements here, and they have all been considered in other chapters. There are four: a safe place to live, the right staff to support, the right training and support for the staff, and individual therapy or care plans to meet identified needs. This can be, and has been, interpreted as possible to meet in an institution. But that doesn't provide a safe place to live, as it is only available for as long as the diagnosis and it is not home, nor is it an emotionally secure base.

Finding a home

A safe place to live needs to be a secure tenancy or an owned home, that is there for life, or as long as is wanted. We have found landlords to be very supportive of the ideas and willing to extend long-term tenancies. We have, at times, purchased the right property if nothing is available on the rental market. Some people have secured housing association properties. The important factor is to find the right property in the right place with the right facilities. So, someone who is very noisy needs a relatively isolated property; someone who is very social needs to be where there are activities and people available. They do need to be ordinary houses on ordinary streets to maintain visibility and access to an ordinary life. Accessing finance for this is another issue, and housing benefit will need to be claimed. Sometimes appointeeship needs to be put in place. At other times, the Court of Protection will have to be engaged to protect the interests of the individual. These issues are all addressed at a low-key level to ensure that there is no further trauma from the experience. Having a safe and reliable place to live is right at the bottom of Maslow's (1968) hierarchy of needs. It is an essential ingredient of an intervention plan that is producing trauma-informed care.

It has been noticeable to me over many years that care homes and such like are sometimes provided with a high standard of furnishings and fittings. They look like hotels, not ordinary homes. Individuals need to be able to live according to their preferences and can feel much better about having found a bargain sofa at the charity shop, than having a super new one delivered that they daren't sit on. Fitting out the home is a gradual process, dependent on the level of interest and ability of the tenant, and needs to be an extension of the identity of the person.

Finding the support staff

Ideally, the staff are appointed for the person. This isn't always possible and, when it isn't, it is good for the individual to meet staff in advance of moving in and to say who they feel comfortable with. If they can, they should be on the appointment panel. Staff may need to be all of one gender, or both. This will have followed from the assessment of need. Women who have been victims of traumatic abuse may need a full female staff group. Men who have had difficult relationships with women may need a total male staff group. Most people can live with both. We ask all our staff to complete a conflict management scale (Roberts, 2003) at interview and we look for people who have a good balance between type A and type B personalities.

Once appointed they receive all their statutory training and then are introduced to trauma-informed care. This includes a training day on "all behaviour has meaning" and then an introduction to the ideas in this book. All behaviour has meaning examines a particular behaviour displayed by an individual from a behavioural, cognitive, psychodynamic, and systems perspective. It helps people to recognise which approach is likely to be most effective for that behaviour with that individual. They are then given a grounding in the emotional developmental model and taught how to provide the right emotional environment for the individual they are going to support. These courses are available online to purchase and could be used by other providers to spread the availability of informed staff for other organisations.

Individual therapy

Many of the people who need trauma-informed care will also need individual therapy to address the traumatic events in their lives. Some will have been multiply traumatised. Some will have suffered trauma in early childhood as well as later. Those who are pre-individuation, which will be the majority, will have struggled to make sense of the world from their infantile position. If they are reasonably able intellectually, they will have suffered multiple rejections and criticisms for what they have done wrong or not done. The adult with learning disability and the emotional age of an infant is difficult to understand and many are thought to be wilful in their refusal to comply or behave. Their inner world is a great source of distress for them and they need help to express their fears and other feelings. Fear is usually the core issue, with other behaviours developing to cover the fear. Some people will engage in aggressive behaviour in order to gain the physical contact of restraint. Identifying the drives and the meaning of the behaviour will have been part of the assessment.

Sessions for therapy can happen in the home or away from home in the therapist's office or therapy room. It needs to be consistent and reliable, providing a secure emotional base to go with the secure physical base. HTP and ORT will have helped to identify the themes that are likely to arise. Weekly or twice-weekly therapy might be needed at first, and will gradually reduce as the seesaw moves from dependence on the therapist to dependence on the home and staff group. By then (maybe two years or so) individuals will be able to look outside of themselves to make relationships with others, and be more able to engage in social activities, make friends, and lead a more ordinary life. The stages of therapy involve the development of trust, facing the past, and then working to a level of resolution that enables the individual to get on with life.

Supporting the staff

It is necessary to support all staff who are working with traumatised people. The level of projections is usually very high, and staff can find their own past distressing experiences are triggered. Or they can find themselves experiencing feelings that they can't identify. At the extreme, the projections make such attacks on linking (Bion, in Symington, 1996 & 1959) that the staff become unable to think straight. This phenomenon has been described well by Bion and requires careful consideration. A communication book is essential so that individuals can work out who is being affected and why. In addition, regular support sessions are needed. This is a place where they can share their thoughts and feelings to help with the resolution of the trauma. A significant feature of traumatised pre-individuated people is their tendency to split. They are not able to tolerate good and bad in themselves, or others, because of their unformed personality and, as a consequence, split the staff group between good and bad. Staff struggle with this, especially if they are branded "bad". This can, of course, be a good thing to be branded "bad" as it means that the distressed person feels safe enough to express negative feelings. However, the staff need to be cared for too, so this happens in the support sessions. When the staff become able to recognise the projections and their meaning, as well as how to help them to stop, they feel better and more able to continue. Losing staff is bad for the individual being supported, as it re-enacts past abandonments, so retaining a staff group is important and is facilitated by the support sessions after the training. It would be beneficial if it became a requirement for all staff working with complex people, to have training in how to provide a therapeutic environment.

Making it happen

Hopefully the leadership from the government departments responsible will listen to those of us who can demonstrate that this model of support and therapy works for those complex individuals who are distressed and emotionally isolated. It does require that there is a will to listen and to allocate the funds in the right place, together with a commitment to supporting the level of skill that is needed in direct support staff. They can be recruited, trained, and supported to do the work. They can't do it without all the ingredients being in place.

Longer term I would hope that the early trauma victims will be identified much sooner and offered what they need. The increased use of fifty-two-week residential schools can only work if the staff in those schools know how to provide the emotional environment that is needed. Many can but it is by no means certain that a child will have a good experience that enables them to move on to adulthood with a sense of self that is robust enough to allow them to live with manageable anxiety.

The work of the special care baby units is much improved and the emotional needs of tiny babies receive much greater attention. This should reduce the incidence of some of the very early trauma. However, there is still not enough support for parents of disabled children in how to help their child, leading to traumatised families who may be more inclined to seek an intervention that takes the child away from the emotional support he or she needs.

There is a growing recognition of the need for secure attachments to facilitate brain development (Gerhardt, 2004). The work described in this book helps us to know what to do to prevent or reduce problems, but, also, what we can do to help when problems have developed. The necessary emotional environment can be provided in the right way at the right time by the right people when the primary process has not been able to do this. We have an obligation to these very distressed people to offer this.

REFERENCES

Alim, N. (2010). Therapeutic progressions of a client and therapist throughout a course of psychodynamic psychotherapy with a man with mild learning disabilities and anger problems. *Advances in Mental Health and Learning Disabilities*, 4: 42–49.

Beail, N. (1998). Psychoanalytic psychotherapy with men with intellectual disabilities: a preliminary outcome study. *British Journal of Medical Psychology*, 71 (1): 1–11.

Beail, N. (2001). Recidivism following psychodynamic psychotherapy amongst offenders with intellectual disabilities. *British Journal of Forensic Practice*, 3 (1): 33–37.

Berry, P. (2003). Psychodynamic therapy and intellectual disabilities: dealing with challenging behaviour. *International Journal of Disability, Development and Education*, 50 (1): 39–51.

Bicknell, J. (1983). The psychotherapy of handicap. *British Journal of Medical Psychology*, 56: 167–178.

Bion, W. R. (1959). Attacks on linking. *International Journal of Psychoanalysis*, 40: 308–315.

Bion, W. R. (1963). *Experience in groups and other papers*. London: Routledge.

Blackman, N. (2003). *Loss and Learning Disability*. London: Worth.

Blackman, N. (2008). The development of an assessment tool for the bereavement needs of people with learning disabilities. *British Journal of Learning Disabilities, 36* (3): 165–170.

Bowlby, J. (1988). *A Secure Base.* London: Routledge.

British Ability Scales, Social Reasoning Scale (3rd edn). London: GL Assessment, 2011.

Brown, H., & Benson, S. (1992). *A Practical Guide to working with People with Learning Disabilities.* London: Hawker.

Crossley, R., & McDonald, A. (1980). *Annie's Coming Out.* Australia: Penguin.

Derogatis, L. R., & Melisaratos, N. (1983). The Brief Symptom Inventory: an introductory report. *Psychological Medicine, 13* (3): 595–605.

Emerson, E. (2001). *Challenging Behaviour: Analysis and Intervention in People with Severe Intellectual Disabilities* (2nd edn). Cambridge: Cambridge University Press.

Fairbairn, W. R. D. (1954). *An Object Relations Theory of the Personality.* Oxford: Basic.

Felce, D. (1986). The Bereweeke Skill-Teaching System: Goal-Setting Checklist for Children. Windsor: NFER-Nelson.

Finkelhor, D. (Ed.) (1984). *Child Sexual Abuse: New Theory and Research.* New York. Free Press.

Firth, G., Elford, H., Leeming, C., & Crabbe, M. (2008). Intensive interaction as a novel approach in social care: care staff's views on the practice change process. *Journal of Applied Research in Intellectual Disabilities, 21* (1): 58–69.

Frankish, P. (1989). Meeting the needs of handicapped people: a psychodynamic approach. *Journal of Mental Deficiency Research, 33:* 407–414.

Frankish, P. (1992). A psychodynamic approach to emotional difficulties within a social framework. *Journal of Intellectual Disability Research, 36:* 559–563.

Frankish, P. (2000). Case Study: A Complex, Multi-element Intervention with a Triple-diagnosed Man. Paper presented at the IASSID World Congress, Seattle. Abstract no 379.

Frankish, P. (2013a). Measuring the emotional development of adults with ID. *Advances in Mental Health and Intellectual Disabilities, 7* (5): 272–276.

Frankish, P. (2013b). Facing emotional pain—a model for working with people with intellectual disabilities and trauma. *ATTACHMENT: New Directions in Psychotherapy and Relational Psychoanalysis, 7:* 276–282.

Freud, S. (1895d). *Studies on Hysteria. S. E., 2.* London: Hogarth.

Gerhardt, S. (2004). *Why Love Matters.* London: Routledge.

Gilbert, P. (2010). *The Compassionate Mind (Compassion Focused Therapy).* London: Constable.

Hollins, S., & Sinason, V. (2000). Psychotherapy, learning disabilities and trauma: new perspectives. *British Journal of Psychiatry, 176*: 32–36.

Jahoda, A., Trower, P., Pert, C., & Finn, D. (2001). Contingent reinforcement or defending the self? A review of evolving models of aggression in people with mild learning disabilities. *British Journal of Medical Psychology, 74*: 305–321.

Kahr, B. (2008). *Sex and the Psyche: The Truth About Our Most Secret Fantasies*. London: Penguin.

Klein, M. (1922). *The psycho-analysis of children*. London: Vintage, 1997.

Klein, M. (1945). *Love, Guilt and Reparation*. London: Vintage, 1998.

Klein, M. (1946). *Envy and Gratitude*. London: Vintage, 1997.

Kroese, B., Dagnan, D., & Loumidis, K. (1997). *Cognitive Behaviour Therapy for People with Learning Disabilities*. London: Routledge.

Larson, F. V., Alim, N., Tsakanikos, E. (2011). Attachment style and mental health in adults with intellectual disability: self reports and reports from carers. *Advances in Mental Health and Intellectual Disabilities 5*: 15–23.

Lindsay, W. R., Michie, A. M., Baty, F. J., Smith, A. H. W., & Miller, S. (1994). The consistency of reports about feelings and emotions from people with intellectual disability. *Journal of Intellectual Disability Research, 38*: 61–66.

Lindsay, W. R., Michie, A. M., Marshall, I., Pitcaithly, D., Broxholme, S., & Hornsby, N. (1996). The effects of behaviour relaxation training on adults with multiple disabilities: a preliminary study on treatment effectiveness. *British Journal of Learning Disabilities, 26*: 44–50.

Lindsay, W. R., Michie, A. M., Whitefield, E., Martin, V., Grieve, A., & Carson, D. (2006). Response patterns on the questionnaire on attitudes consistent with sexual offending in groups of sex offenders with intellectual disabilities. *Journal of Applied Research in Intellectual Disabilities, 19*: 47–53.

Mahler, M., Pine, F., & Bergman, A. (1979). *The Psychological Birth of the Human Infant*. New York: Basic.

Malan, D. H. (2001). *Individual Psychotherapy and the Science of Psychodynamics* (2nd edn). London: Arnold.

Martin, J. P., & Evans, D. (1984). *Hospitals in Trouble*. Oxford: Blackwell.

Maslow, A. (1968). *Towards a Psychology of Being*. New York: Van Nostrand.

Osgood, T. (2004). *Suit You, Sir? Challenging Behaviour in Learning Disability Services*. Canterbury: Tizard Centre, University of Kent.

Parkes, G., Mukherjee, R. A. S., Karagianni, E., Attavar, R., Sinason, V., & Hollins, S. (2007). Referrals to an intellectual disability psychotherapy service in an inner city catchment area—a retrospective case notes study. *Journal of Applied Research in Intellectual Disabilities, 20*: 373–378.

Perry, J., Felce, D., Allen, D., & Meek, A. (2011). *Resettlement outcome for people with severe challenging behaviour moving from institutional to community living. Journal of Applied Research in Intellectual Disabilities, 24*: 1–17.

Phillipson, H. (1988). The use of O.R.T. as a facilitator of maturational process: some implications for a range of applications with special reference to subliminal activation of preconscious processing. *British Journal of Projective Psychology, 33* (1): 84–105.

Prouty, G., & Cronwall, M. (1990). Psychotherapeutic approaches in the treatment of depression in mentally retarded adults. In: Dosen, A. & Menolascino, F. (Eds.), *Depression in Mentally Retarded Children and Adults* (pp. 281–293). Leiden: Logon.

Prouty, G. (1994). *Theoretical Evolutions in Person-Centered/Experiential Therapy: Applications to Schizophrenic and Retarded Psychoses.* Westport, CT: Praeger.

Roberts, M. (2003). *Conflict-management style survey.* The Pfeiffer Library Vol 5 (3rd edn). Chichester: Wiley.

Rogers, C. (1951). *Client-centred Therapy: Its Current Practice, Implications and Theory.* London: Constable.

Roth, A., & Fonagy, P. (2005). *What works for whom?* New York: Guilford.

Royal College of Psychiatrists (2004). *Psychotherapy and Learning Disability Report.* London: RCP.

Sinason, V. (1992). *Mental Handicap and the Human Condition: New Approaches from Tavistock.* London: Free Association, 2010.

Sturmey, P. (2008). *How to Teach Verbal Behaviour.* Austin, TX: Pro Ed.

Symington, J., & Symington, N. (1996). *The Clinical Thinking of Wilfred Bion.* London: Routledge.

Taylor, J. L., Novaco, R.W., Gillmer, B., & Thorne, I. (2002). Cognitive behavioural treatment of anger intensity among offenders with intellectual disability. *Journal of Applied Research in Intellectual Disability 15*: 151–165.

van den Broek, M. D., & Bradshaw, C. M. (1994). Detection of acquired deficits in general intelligence using the National Adult Reading Test and Raven's Standard Progressive Matrices. *British Journal of Clinical Psychology, 33*: 509–515.

Viera, A. J., & Garrett, J. M. (2005). Understanding inter-observer agreement: the kappa statistic. *Family Medicine, 37* (5): 360–363.

Wechsler, D. (1939). *The Measurement of Adult Intelligence.* Baltimore, MD: Williams and Wilkins.

Willner, P., Rose, J., Jahoda, A., Kroese, B. S., Felce, D., Cohen, D., MacMahon, P., Stimpson, A., Rose, N., Gillespie, D., Shead, J., Lammie, C., Woodgate, C., Townson, J., Nuttall, J., & Hood, K. (2013). Group-based cognitive-behavioural anger management for people with mild to moderate intellectual disabilities: cluster randomised control trial. *British Journal of Psychiatry, 203*: 288–296.

Winnicott, D. W. (1971a). *Playing and Reality*. London: Routledge.

Winnicott, D. W. (1965). *Maturational Processes and the Facilitating Environment*. London: Karnac, 1990.

Winnicott, D. W. (1971b). *The Piggle*. London: Hogarth.

Winnicott, D. W. (1973). *The Child, the Family and the Outside World*. Middlesex: Penguin.

Winnicott, D. W., & Winnicott, C. (1990). *Home is Where we Start From*. Middlesex: Penguin.

Wolfensberger, W. (1972). *The Principle of Normalisation in Human Services*. Toronto, Canada: National Institute on Mental Retardation.

INDEX